A Team Approach to

Behaviour Management

A Team Approach to Behaviour Management

A TRAINING GUIDE FOR SENCOs WORKING WITH TEACHING ASSISTANTS

CHRIS DERRINGTON AND BARRY GROOM

P·C·P

Paul Chapman Publishing

First published 2004

Paul Chapman Publishing
A SAGE Publications Company
1 Oliver's Yard
55 City Road
London EC1Y 1SP

SAGE Publications Inc
2455 Teller Road
Thousand Oaks, California 91320

SAGE Publications India Pvt Ltd
B-42, Panchsheel Enclave
Post Box 4109
New Delhi 100 017

Library of Congress Control Number: 2003115337

A catalogue record for this book is available from the British Library

ISBN 1-4129-0035-2
ISBN 1-4129-0036-0 (pbk)

Typeset by Dorwyn Ltd, Rowlands Castle, Hants
Printed by Cromwell Press, Trowbridge, Wilts

Contents

Acknowledgements

This training guide is based on courses that the authors have developed and delivered as part of University College Northampton's programme of continued professional development for teaching assistants (TAs) and special educational needs co-ordinators (SENCOs) in Northamptonshire and surrounding authorities. The materials have been revised and updated over a number of years, largely as a result of the helpful feedback we receive from those people for whom this training is targeted – the teaching assistants and SENCOs themselves. We would like to thank these individuals for their boundless enthusiasm and dedication, which never ceases to amaze us!

Chris Derrington would also like to acknowledge colleagues from Northamptonshire Local Education Authority including Jan Martin, Dave Stott, Alison Cuthill, Maggie Lyndsey, Tim Bunn, Judy Jennings, Clarissa Prior-Jones, Owen Walker, Mandy Owen and Marian Keenaghan for their contributions in the early stages of course development.

Finally, the authors would like to express their sincere gratitude to colleagues at CeSNER (Centre for Special Needs Education and Research) University College Northampton for their support in this project. In particular, we would like to thank Professor Richard Rose for his continued encouragement and guidance.

Introduction

This training guide has been developed and written primarily for SENCOs in primary, secondary and special schools who manage the work of teaching assistants. It will also be of interest to other senior teachers or advisory staff who lead training in the area of behaviour management.

There has been a substantial increase in the use of teaching assistants across all phases over recent years and although off-site training opportunities for them have steadily developed, our experience shows that it is training in behaviour management that schools and teaching assistants themselves believe to be a high priority. Special Educational Needs Co-ordinators are now becoming the lead managers of teaching assistants within their schools and are taking increasing responsibility for areas of in-house training on special educational needs (SEN) and whole-school issues.

This book is designed to provide a structure for the SENCO to deliver team-training sessions with their teaching assistants in the area of behaviour management. The emphasis is on a planned team approach to problem-solving and mutual support within the context of whole-school development. Each unit is designed to promote a reflective approach in understanding pupil behaviour and in the development of personal and professional skills.

The book has been designed to provide the SENCO with all the training materials, photocopy resources, activities, tasks and discussion topics they need to deliver the programme. Each unit follows the same structure and format, and contains suggestions for further reading. In addition, each unit provides materials and ideas for follow-up work including reflective logs and planning sheets.

The units in this training guide can be used in a flexible way and in any order of preference. Users may wish to follow the format exactly as it appears in the book or select units in a different order. The training can be delivered in small chunks (suitable for twilight sessions or team meetings) or over a longer period (for example, on staff training days).

From our experience of delivering courses based on these materials, we have found that teaching assistants have gained considerably in confidence and knowledge, and have built a firm base for their personal and professional development in supporting the positive management of behaviour across the school.

Chris Derrington

Barry Groom

Knowing our Whole-School Behaviour Policy

UNIT OBJECTIVES

This unit provides a format for the SENCO to promote a positive and proactive whole-school approach to managing behaviour. The focus of the unit is on the school's own policy – its aims, expectations and responses to develop a learning community.

The objectives of the unit are:

- to highlight a collegiate and consistent approach to managing behaviour
- to provide information on the school's systems, procedures and approaches
- to set activities for the teaching assistant team to reflect on aspects of their practice.

The session activities are designed to support the teaching assistant to:

- identify personal and professional qualities that contribute to confident and effective practice
- understand the importance of the school culture and ethos in promoting positive behaviour
- identify roles and responsibilities and support systems
- identify school procedures
- plan and respond appropriately including the reporting and recording of incidents.

PRIOR TO THE SESSION

Distribute copies of your Whole-School Behaviour Policy to your teaching assistant team at least a week before this session to give them the opportunity to familiarize themselves with the general outline of the policy. Ask them to jot down any particular areas for clarification.

SESSION MATERIALS AND AUDIO/VISUAL AIDS

- Whole-School Behaviour Policy.
- Overhead projector.
- Flip-chart sheets and pens.

UNIT 1 RESOURCES

OHT 1.1: Elements of the Whole-School Behaviour Policy
OHT 1.2: Ways in which teaching assistants support the positive ethos of the school
OHT 1.3: Personal and professional skills of teaching assistants in supporting a positive approach to behaviour
Activity 1.1: Responding to challenging behaviour
Activity 1.2: Six scenarios for discussion
Team post-session plan
Individual post-session plan
Reflective log

NOTES FOR SENCO/TRAINER: OUR WHOLE-SCHOOL BEHAVIOUR POLICY

The Whole-School Behaviour Policy not only sets out the school's planned systems of managing behaviour it also implicitly sets out its *aims, values* and *expectations.* It is the framework for a proactive, positive and consistent approach to support a process of enabling learning in an ordered, safe and secure environment. Good practice suggests it will have been developed from a consensus, led by the headteacher and governing body involving detailed discussions with school staff, parents, pupils and often with outside agencies and community users of the school. It will have been informed by both national and local guidelines and will set out how the school operates as a *learning community* – detailing both rights and responsibilities and the expectations of people living and learning together. It will promote an inclusive ethos and be cross-referenced to all other whole-school policies that reflect the school's approach to equal opportunities, special educational needs and the recognition of diversity and differences.

To be most effective, the policy will at all times be 'active' – i.e. seen to be in practice inside and outside the classroom, and known by all members of the school community including parents, governors and visitors to the school. Aspects of the policy will be displayed in classrooms and highlighted on noticeboards around the school.

Within this framework the Whole-School Behaviour Policy will outline the following interlinked elements, offer guidance and provide examples of desired and intended practices.

- involvement in planning, assessment and target setting
- extra-curricular activities, lunch and homework clubs
- additional classroom support.

For parents:

- designated person for relating information, discussing progress and concerns
- access to parent support groups
- involvement with governors.

THE SPECIFIC RESPONSIBILITIES OF DIFFERENT MEMBERS OF STAFF

The policy will outline responsibilities that all members of staff have in managing behaviour and promoting positive relationships throughout the school. Designated members of staff, members of the senior management team and governor representatives will have specific responsibilities.

LINKS TO OTHER SCHOOL POLICIES

The Whole-School Behaviour Policy will be cross-referenced with a range of other policies, most notably with the school's policies on child protection, bullying, race equality, physical intervention and special educational needs policy.

FURTHER READING

Ayers, H., Clarke, D. and Murray, A. (2000) *Perspectives on Behaviour: A Practical Guide to Effective Interventions for Teachers*. London: David Fulton.

Mosely, J. (1993) *Turn your School Around*. Wisbech: LDA.

Porter, L. (2000) *Behaviour in Schools: Theory and Practice for Teachers*. Milton Keynes: Open University Press.

STRUCTURE OF THE SESSION

The OHT and activity resources for Unit 1 can be used in any sequence.

A suggested structure is as follows:

Notes for OHT 1.1

ELEMENTS OF THE WHOLE-SCHOOL
BEHAVIOUR POLICY

Emphasize the importance of a collegiate
approach, and how each element within the
policy is interlinked. Give examples of how the
aims of the school are illustrated and under-
pinned by the *ethos and culture* of the school.
Illustrate any specific points within the elements that are specifically relevant to your
school development or training needs. Use this
first part of the session as information giving,
providing an overview of the policy.

ELEMENTS OF OUR WHOLE-SCHOOL BEHAVIOUR POLICY

- AIMS OF THE SCHOOL

- THE SCHOOL'S EXPECTATIONS OF BEHAVIOUR

- HOW IT PROMOTES POSITIVE BEHAVIOUR

- RIGHTS AND RESPONSIBILITIES

- CODE OF CONDUCT/RULES

- REWARDS AND SANCTIONS

- THE SYSTEMS FOR MANAGING BEHAVIOUR

- THE SUPPORT NETWORKS FOR STAFF, PUPILS AND PARENTS

- THE SPECIFIC RESPONSIBILITIES OF DIFFERENT MEMBERS OF STAFF

Notes for OHT 1.2

WAYS IN WHICH TEACHING ASSISTANTS
SUPPORT THE POSITIVE ETHOS
OF THE SCHOOL

OHT 1.2 identifies some of the areas of work in which the team demonstrates its contribution to a positive ethos in and around the school. Ask the team to add other aspects of their work to those displayed on the OHT. Collate responses on the flip chart and pin it up.

WAYS IN WHICH TEACHING ASSISTANTS SUPPORT THE POSITIVE ETHOS OF THE SCHOOL

Supporting a positive classroom atmosphere

Resolving conflict

Being an adult role model

Working as a member of a team

Highlighting positive behaviour

Planning and implementing individual behaviour programmes

Supporting and assisting around the school: assemblies, playgrounds, breaks, etc.

Notes for OHT 1.3

PERSONAL AND PROFESSIONAL
SKILLS OF TEACHING ASSISTANTS IN
SUPPORTING A POSITIVE APPROACH
TO BEHAVIOUR

OHT 1.3 further identifies many of the personal and professional skills the team will use on a day-to-day basis in supporting pupils. Highlight examples from practice. Discuss and share good practice.

PERSONAL AND PROFESSIONAL SKILLS OF TEACHING ASISSTANTS

- Showing trust and respect

- Being approachable and welcoming

- Being fair and consistent

- Showing understanding and empathy

- Appreciating difference and diversity

- Establishing positive relationships with pupils

- Being aware of school systems and policies

▶ ACTIVITY 1.1: RESPONDING TO CHALLENGING BEHAVIOUR

In this activity members of the team are asked to rank specific behaviours according to the response on a continuum. **(A)** normal TA management of the classroom **(B)** referring to class teacher or **(C)** direct to senior member of staff.

After discussion in pairs ask members to feed back their ideas.

Discuss the responses, emphasizing to team members how in many circumstances (a) knowledge of the child, (b) the context of the behaviour and (c) planned programmes of intervention may influence the level of response.

How would you rank these (**A, B** or **C**) according to the level of appropriate response? (**A**) normal TA management of the classroom (**B**) referring to class teacher or (**C**) direct to senior member of staff.

1. Spitting at another pupil   A   B   C

2. Racist comments   A   B   C

3. Deliberately pushing another pupil   A   B   C

4. Out of seat unnecessarily   A   B   C

5. Refusal to undertake task   A   B   C

6. Continually talking during lesson   A   B   C

7. Using inappropriate language   A   B   C

8. Fighting in the playground   A   B   C

9. Destroying own work   A   B   C

10. Stealing items from other pupils   A   B   C

© A Team Approach to Behaviour Management by Chris Derrington & Barry Groom, Paul Chapman Publishing, 2004.

▶ ACTIVITY 1.2: SIX SCENARIOS FOR DISCUSSION IN
SMALL GROUPS

Six different scenarios are outlined in which team members are
asked to consider what intervention they would make. Two scenario cards can be given to each group to discuss.

1. YOU HAVE A NEW TEACHING ASSISTANT JOINING THE TEAM

How might you offer support?

What specific aspects of the behaviour policy would be essential for a new member of staff to be aware of?

(Think back to when you started – what did you need to know?)

2. RECOGNIZING ACHIEVEMENT

A pupil you have been working with has made really good progress in improving aspects of their behaviour.

You feel that this should be celebrated and that the pupil should receive recognition for their achievement.

In what format might this recognition be shown?

© A Team Approach to Behaviour Management by Chris Derrington & Barry Groom, Paul Chapman Publishing, 2004.

3. PROCEDURES FOR SUPPORT

A pupil with behavioural difficulties with whom you have been working for some time leaves the school site without permission. You find out that he has fallen out with other pupils during the lunch break.

What course of action would you take?

4. REPORTING AND RECORDING INCIDENTS

You have witnessed an incident in the playground.

Two pupils have argued over the ownership of a personal stereo player. One pupil insists that the other pupil swapped the item with him for a toy. During the argument the personal stereo player has been dropped and is broken. Both pupils are upset. The school rules state that pupils should not bring personal belongings into school.

How do you deal with the incident? How is it reported and recorded?

5. DEVISING A REWARD SYSTEM

You have been asked to devise an individual REWARD system to support the targets for a pupil with behavioural difficulties. You have developed a good relationship with the pupil.

The pupil has difficulties in sustaining concentration, staying on task and remaining in his seat. He often distracts other pupils and calls out inappropriately.

It is important to retain consistency and fairness within the framework of the Whole-School Behaviour Policy. What might be an appropriate reward system to support the pupil to achieve his targets?

6. DEVELOPING FRIENDSHIP SKILLS

You have observed that a new pupil in school is isolated during playtime and appears not to be involved in forming friendships.

How might you respond to this situation?

What resources/support within the school would you seek?

What interventions might be used?

Who might be involved?

TEAM POST-SESSION PLAN

UNIT 1: KNOWING OUR WHOLE-SCHOOL BEHAVIOUR POLICY

What aspects of the Whole-School Behaviour Policy do we need to work on as a team?

1.

2.

3.

Actions to be taken:

INDIVIDUAL POST-SESSION PLAN

UNIT 1: KNOWING OUR WHOLE-SCHOOL BEHAVIOUR POLICY

Task for the next session:

REFLECTIVE LOG

UNIT 1: KNOWING OUR WHOLE-SCHOOL BEHAVIOUR POLICY

How does your knowledge and understanding of the Whole-School Behaviour Policy help you in your teaching assistant role?

What implications might it have for future practice?

Understanding our Role as Teaching Assistants in Supporting Behaviour

UNIT OBJECTIVES

This unit explores the specific tasks and roles undertaken by the teaching assistant in supporting pupil behaviour and discusses the personal qualities and professional skills that underpin them.

The objectives of the unit are:

- to consider the nature and scope of the teaching assistant role in supporting behaviour
- to reflect on the importance of positive relationships with pupils and teachers and explore ways of developing these further
- to identify tensions and develop solutions through problem-solving activities
- to promote a consistency of approach for teaching assistant practice in supporting behaviour across the school.

The session activities are designed to support the teaching assistant to:

- understand and reflect upon the many different facets of their role in supporting pupils with behaviour difficulties
- consider some of the personal qualities and professional skills needed to fulfil their role
- reflect upon their own future professional development.

PRIOR TO THE SESSION

Team members should complete the pre-session task sheet 'Aspects of my role'. Team members should write down an example of one activity that they have been involved in over the last week in each of the corresponding sections.

SESSION MATERIALS AND AUDIO/VISUAL AIDS

- Overhead projector.
- Flip-chart sheets and pens.

UNIT 2 RESOURCES

Pre-session task: aspects of my role

OHT 2.1: The range of tasks teaching assistants undertake in supporting behaviour

OHT 2.2: Ways in which teaching assistants support behaviour

OHT 2.3: The qualities and attributes of teaching assistants

Activity 2.1: Working as a team

Team post-session plan

Individual post-session plan

Reflective log

PRE-SESSION TASK

ASPECTS OF MY ROLE

Write down ONE activity that you have been involved in over the last week
in each of the sections:

Support to promote the ethos and policies of the school

Support for staff

Support for the curriculum

Support for promoting pupil development and welfare

Support for parent/carer

Support for resources

Support for planning, record keeping and administrative tasks

NOTES FOR SENCO/TRAINER

Supporting pupils with behavioural difficulties can be one of the most challenging roles that teaching assistants can undertake. It involves utilizing a range of professional and personal skills, and applying them across a variety of contexts and situations to engage and draw within the learning process pupils who may exhibit extremes of emotions and behaviours. Within the inclusive classroom it is likely that teaching assistants will be supporting pupils who have a range of complex needs including pupils with specific learning difficulties, physical and sensory impairments, social, emotional and behavioural difficulties, attention deficit hyperactivity disorder (ADHD) and pupils who have communication difficulties including autism and Asperger's syndrome.

Those pupils that have been identified as having special educational needs will be supported by planned programmes of intervention including individual education plans (IEPs).

The planned programme and IEP will outline the difficulties the pupil is experiencing, detail differentiated strategies and resources to be employed and set realistic targets for the pupil to aim for over a given period of time.

The essential role of the teaching assistant is to provide, under the guidance of the teacher, the additional support required to enable the pupil to achieve.

DEVELOPING POSITIVE RELATIONSHIPS WITH PUPILS

Children are more likely to learn at their best when they can form relationships with key adults in their lives who treat them with respect, who can demonstrate that they care for their welfare when they are troubled or anxious and who make efforts to understand them as individuals.

Individual support and guidance for children, particularly for those that have social and emotional factors related to their behaviour difficulties, can undoubtedly make a positive impact in encouraging them further forward to take risks in their learning and relationships. Some pupils may have had previous negative and confused experiences in their interactions with adults and will need a sympathetic and supportive adult mentor who can patiently help them to build up their confidence and trust. Children with behaviour difficulties often hold negative views about themselves and about their abilities and achievements. They can often have an inner view of themselves as a 'bad' or 'stupid' person; a view they have construed from what they have heard, or interpreted, from the feedback given to them by adults about their actions. Children who constantly hear negative comments about themselves will come to believe that they cannot be a good or worthwhile person. It is essential in our interactions with children that we demonstrate our acceptance of them as worthwhile individuals with positive qualities.

We can all recall from our own childhood those adults who had a particular positive impact on us. We remember them because they were *significant* adults to us, and our interactions and experiences with them have contributed in part to who we are as adults. We will particularly hold those people in high regard who we felt recognized the things we did well and who encouraged and challenged us to try our best. The personal qualities, attributes and values held by the person are likely to have been significant factors in why we responded positively to them.

The teaching assistant can undertake an important proactive role in initiating po
interactions with pupils by:

- saying hello and greeting them by name and with a smile when they
  arrive at school
- engaging them in conversation about everyday things
- asking how they feel
- inquiring about their interests and hobbies
- taking an interest in their day-to-day lives
- engaging their interest and attention through humour
- giving them encouragement
- noticing if they are troubled or upset
- saying something positive about them
- showing trust by giving them responsibilities around the school.

These everyday positive interactions – giving specific attention and notice and validating the pupil's presence – can be a non-threatening starting point to engage further with the pupil in both formal and informal contexts around the school.

THE RANGE OF TASKS TEACHING ASSISTANTS UNDERTAKE IN SUPPORTING BEHAVIOUR

Teaching assistants undertake a range of both direct and indirect tasks in their role to support behaviour and will have an input and involvement in the following interrelated areas:

- support to promote the ethos and policies of the school
- support for staff
- support for the curriculum
- support for promoting pupil development and welfare
- support for parents/carers
- support for resources
- support for planning, record-keeping and administrative tasks.

Examples of specific tasks undertaken by the teaching assistant to support behaviour might include:

- settling the child into school
- sitting close by to spot 'triggers' and prevent difficulties
- keeping the pupil on track
- ensuring the pupil has correct equipment
- giving positive attention
- giving reminders about behaviour targets
- modelling and teaching new behaviour
- observing behaviour to gather information

- recording on- and off-target behaviours
- resolving conflicts between students
- calming situations which are becoming heated
- monitoring or tracking a student throughout a day
- establishing a relationship with a student and providing a listening ear
- speaking on the child's behalf
- keeping records and reporting back to the teacher
- contributing to evaluation and review
- meeting parents/carers to discuss progress.

KEY SKILLS AND KNOWLEDGE FOR TEACHING ASSISTANTS SUPPORTING BEHAVIOUR

Teaching assistants will have a range of:

- behaviour management strategies
- skills in observation and recording
- skills in keeping records and contributing to reports
- strategies to develop and maintain relationships
- skills in writing and evaluating targets
- skills in communicating effectively

and knowledge of:

- school behaviour policies and practice
- information about the child from IEPs, individual behaviour plans (IBPs) and pastoral support plans (PSPs)
- line management and systems for support and appraisal
- responsibilities and role
- daily school information
- child protection procedures.

PERSONAL QUALITIES OF TEACHING ASSISTANTS

Teaching assistants are likely to have a wide range of personal skills that they bring to their role including:

- patience
- a sense of fairness
- consistency
- sensitivity
- ability to learn from mistakes
- flexibility
- versatility

- positive attitudes
- friendliness
- sense of humour
- enthusiasm
- confidence
- assertiveness
- 'broad shoulders'
- belief that children can develop and change.

WORKING AS PART OF A TEAM

Good practice in effective schools indicates there are a range of features that are evident in teams working together successfully. These include members of the team working to common goals, sharing the same values and having high standards and expectations within their work. Within successful teams planning and reviewing is a collaborative task that involves input from all members of the team.

FURTHER READING

Balshaw, M. and Farrell, P. (2002) *Teaching Assistants: Practical Strategies for Effective Classroom Support*. London: David Fulton.

Fox, G. (2001) *Supporting Children with Behaviour Difficulties*. London: David Fulton.

STRUCTURE OF THE SESSION

A suggested structure for the session is as follows.

Notes for OHT 2.1

THE RANGE OF TASKS TEACHING ASSISTANTS UNDERTAKE IN SUPPORTING BEHAVIOUR

Use OHT 2.1 as a stimulus for the team to discuss the range and type of tasks they undertake in the areas mapped out. Refer to the completed pre-session task sheets and ask team members to give examples. In small groups ask team members to think of as many specific aspects of their role they can group under each heading and to write them on flip-chart sheets. When completed, display the sheets and discuss with the team.

Are they aware of the range of the tasks they undertake? Are they cognizant of the 'big picture'? Do they feel more confident in some areas of their role than others?

THE RANGE OF TASKS TEACHING ASSISTANTS UNDERTAKE IN SUPPORTING BEHAVIOUR

- Support to promote the ethos and policies of the school

- Support for staff

- Support for the curriculum

- Support for promoting pupil development and welfare

- Support for parents/carers

- Support for resources

- Support for planning, record-keeping and administrative tasks

Notes for OHT 2.2

OHT 2.2: WAYS IN WHICH TEACHING
ASSISTANTS SUPPORT BEHAVIOUR

Use OHT 2.2 to discuss the range of ways the
team supports behaviour across the school. In
small groups ask the team members to add to
the list using flip-chart sheets. Display the
sheets and discuss. Do team members feel
more confident in some areas rather than
others?

WAYS IN WHICH TEACHING ASSISTANTS SUPPORT BEHAVIOUR

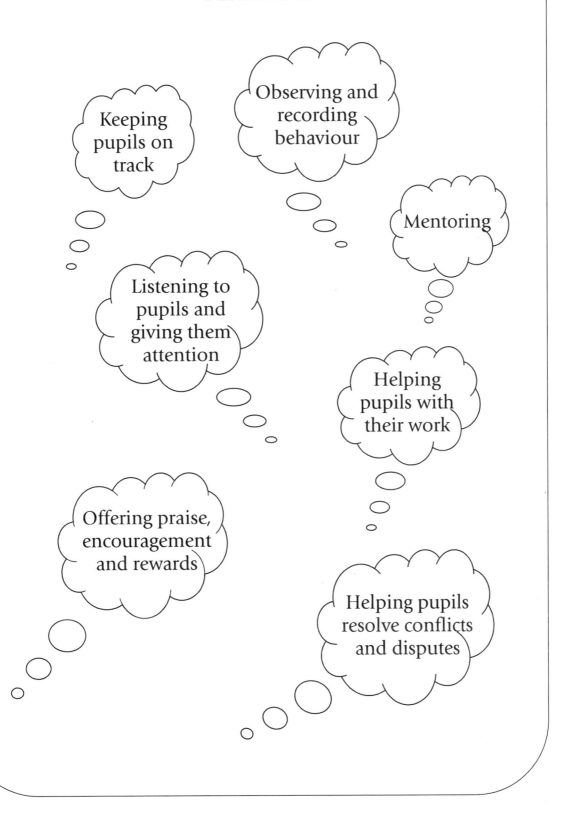

Notes for OHT 2.3

OHT 2.3: QUALITIES AND ATTRIBUTES OF TEACHING ASSISTANTS

Display OHT 2.3 and discuss with the team the range of personal qualities and attributes. Explain the meaning and relevance of 'significant others'. Ask members of the team to share with a partner recollections of teachers/relatives who influenced them positively when they were children. What were the qualities and attributes of these people? Are they similar qualities and attributes teaching assistants bring to their role?

QUALITIES AND ATTRIBUTES OF TEACHING ASSISTANTS

Patience
Friendliness
Fairness

Listening
skills

Positive
attitudes

Consistency
Sensitivity
Flexibility

Versatility
Enthusiasm

Ability to
learn from
mistakes

Confidence
Assertiveness

▶ ACTIVITY 2.1: WORKING AS A TEAM

Ask the team to work in small groups to complete the activity. What other headings might there be? Use flip-chart sheets to display all the examples given showing how the team works effectively and collaboratively together.

What aspects do the team think they are particularly adept at? What areas need developing?

Write an example under each heading that demonstrates the ways the team works collaboratively and effectively.

Communicating

Planning and reviewing

Discussing problems

Sharing successes

Supporting each other

TEAM POST-SESSION PLAN

UNIT 2: UNDERSTANDING OUR ROLE AS TEACHING ASSISTANTS IN SUPPORTING BEHAVIOUR

What aspects of the role do we need to work on as a team?

1.

2.

3.

Actions to be taken:

INDIVIDUAL POST-SESSION PLAN

UNIT 2: UNDERSTANDING OUR ROLE AS TEACHING ASSISTANTS IN SUPPORTING BEHAVIOUR

Task for the next session

REFLECTIVE LOG

UNIT 2: UNDERSTANDING OUR ROLE AS TEACHING ASSISTANTS IN SUPPORTING BEHAVIOUR

What specific aspects of my role do I need to develop?

What implications might it have for future practice?

Are We a Listening Team?

UNIT OBJECTIVES

The focus of this unit is the development of listening skills for more effective communication with pupils and colleagues.

The objectives of the unit are:

- to enhance active listening skills and raise self-awareness
- to illustrate the relationship between interpersonal communication, self-esteem, motivation and behaviour
- to demonstrate the importance of effective listening when supporting pupils and working in partnership with colleagues.

The session activities are designed to support the teaching assistant to:

- evaluate his/her own listening ability
- identify and reduce obstructions to effective listening
- rehearse and improve active listening skills
- become more effective communicators.

PRIOR TO THE SESSION

At some point during the week before this session, participants should choose one of the following: an assembly/staff briefing meeting/television news programme/lesson introduction. The task is to really focus in and listen attentively for a period of 15 minutes. On the *following day*, participants should write down all that they remember about what they heard during that assembly/meeting/television news programme/lesson introduction.

SESSION MATERIALS AND AUDIO/VISUAL AIDS

- Overhead projector.
- Flip chart and pens.
- Cue cards for Activity 3.2.

UNIT 3 RESOURCES

OHT 3.1: Types of listening
OHT 3.2: Good listening skills
Activity 3.1: Sharing experiences
Activity 3.2: Inhibitors to listening
Activity 3.3: Rehearsing good listening skills
Team post-session plan
Individual post-session plan
Reflective log

NOTES FOR SENCO/TRAINER: ARE WE A LISTENING TEAM?

The development of interpersonal skills is an important component of our courses for teachers and teaching assistants. The rationale for this is that much of our own behaviour can and will influence the behaviour and responses of the pupils with whom we work. There is no getting away from the fact that, sometimes, the behaviour of certain adults in school has the effect of winding pupils up, alienating/demotivating them or triggering an aggressive outburst. Unfortunately, it is not just pupils that are capable of rudeness, sarcasm and verbal abuse. (These hostile styles of behaviour management are explored more fully in Unit 7.) Effective managers of behaviour tend to be those individuals who look at and analyse their own behaviour (as well as that of the pupils) with a view to developing and improving their own interpersonal skills. A focus on assertiveness skills and effective verbal/non-verbal communication are covered in Units 6 and 7. This unit focuses predominantly on listening skills which, although central to the work of the teaching assistant, are rarely taught in any systematic way.

A large proportion of the teaching assistant's time in school is spent listening, not only to the content of lessons and to teacher instructions, but also to pupils' ideas, anxieties, concerns, complaints and opinions. Both aspects are important, but require different types of listening skills, and the session will be used to clarify this concept. From our experience, teaching assistants often develop positive and trusting relationships with the pupils they support. It may well be the teaching assistant who first becomes alerted to personal problems such as bullying, abuse or family difficulties. It is important to spend some time in this session, therefore, clarifying school procedures for disclosure and child protection. It may be helpful to devise four or five scenarios of disclosure for discussion in the group. It should also be emphasized that effective communication with colleagues (as well as with pupils) is an essential ingredient for successful learning support. As discussed in Unit 2, good working relationships between teachers and assistants depend on clear lines of communication and an understanding and appreciation of one another's position. Understanding another person's point of view can reduce the potential for interpersonal conflict.

FURTHER READING

Greenhalgh, P. (1994) *Emotional Growth and Learning*. London: Routledge

MacGrath, M. (2000) *The Art of Peaceful Teaching in the Primary School*. London: David Fulton.

STRUCTURE OF THE SESSION

A suggested structure is as follows: first, it is important to make the distinction between 'hearing' and 'listening'. The former is a passive sensory response, the latter is a skill that can be honed and developed. Secondly, there should be some discussion about 'types' of listening.

DIFFERENT TYPES OF LISTENING

OHT 3.1 identifies some different types of listening and explanatory notes follow.

INFORMATIVE LISTENING

Where your aim is to concentrate on the message being given. This may be the content of a lesson, directions, instructions, etc. Ask the team whether they use any strategies to help them focus or retain information in this context. Are there any ideas here for helping pupils with auditory learning difficulties?

The pre-session task is a useful awareness raising exercise that should:

- illustrate that informative listening is HARD WORK
- confirm that it is difficult to retain information we have listened to
- reveal some of the obstructions to effective listening
- remind colleagues how hard it must be for pupils to keep up their concentration levels all day long.

Ask colleagues which parts they found it easiest to remember and why. Feedback from this introductory activity could lead on to a sharing of experiences and a discussion about preferred learning styles. As a team, discuss the extent to which visual or kinaesthetic learners' needs are recognized and addressed in classrooms.

APPRECIATIVE LISTENING

Where the listener gains pleasure/satisfaction from listening to a certain type of music for example. Appreciative sources might also include particular charismatic speakers or entertainers. These are personal preferences and may have been shaped through our experiences and expectations.

CRITICAL LISTENING

Where the listener may be trying to weigh up whether the speaker is credible, whether the message being given is logical and whether they are being duped or manipulated by the speaker. This is the type of listening that we may adopt when faced with an offer or sales pitch that requires a decision from us.

DISCRIMINATIVE LISTENING

Where the listener is able to identify and distinguish inferences or emotions through the speaker's change in voice tone, their use of pause, etc. Some people are extremely sensitive in this way, while others are less able to pick up these subtle cues. Where the listener may recognize and pinpoint a specific engine fault, a familiar laugh from a crowded theatre or their own child's cry in a noisy playground. This ability may be affected by hearing impairment.

EMPATHIC LISTENING

Where the listener tends to listen rather than talk. Their non-verbal behaviour indicates that the listener is attending to what is being said. The emphasis is on understanding the speaker's feelings and being supportive and patient. The remaining exercise and paired activities are designed to demonstrate the advantages of empathic listening and to highlight a range of obstructions that may prevent us from being effective listeners.

TYPES OF LISTENING

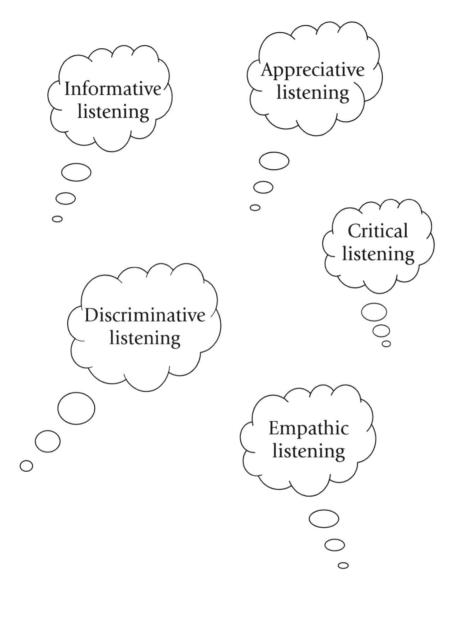

► ACTIVITY 3.1: SHARING EXPERIENCES

Ask participants to think of a time when they felt that someone really listened to them in this (empathic) way. How did it make them feel? Discuss in pairs. The main reward for the speaker is that it often reaffirms their sense of self-worth. It can help to raise self-esteem. This has direct implications for our work with pupils. Now ask them to think of a time when they felt that a person was not listening to them when they had something important or significant to say. How did that make them feel? Ask for feedback.

▶ ACTIVITY 3.2: INHIBITORS TO LISTENING

Divide the team into pairs and give a cue card to one member of each pair. The cue card should be read by the recipient but it must not be shared with their partner.

The person without the card should then proceed to tell their partner all about the last vacation they had. The listeners respond according to the instructions on the card. After a few minutes, stop the exercise and give a different cue card to the other partner in each pair and then reverse the activity. Ask the team how they felt when they were telling their stories.

On a flip chart, put the heading 'Listening inhibitors' and ask the team to feed back their observations. Make a list of the obstructions or inhibitors to effective listening. These might include: lack of concentration, lack of interest, distraction, egocentricity, bias, impatience, inappropriate body language, impulsiveness, etc.

Say nothing throughout but smile weakly, nod from time to time and occasionally laugh half-heartedly. After a few moments:
– stifle a yawn
– close your eyes for a few seconds
– yawn openly
– straighten your back or roll your shoulders as though feeling stiff or uncomfortable.

Listen and appear interested at first but then hijack the conversation and refer everything back to your own experiences:
– 'Oh I've been there and … '
– 'That's what happened to my brother and he … '
– 'Something even worse happened to me … '
– 'You should have gone to … '

Listen and appear interested at first but then allow yourself to become distracted by another person's story nearby. Act as though their story is more interesting than your partner's.
– Look towards the other pair from time to time.
– Smile or laugh at something they say.
– Turn back to your partner and say, 'Sorry, I missed that.'

Listen enthusiastically. Then start to anticipate what your partner is going to say. Finish their sentences for them and say things like:
– 'Oh and I suppose that you had to come home early.'
– 'Don't tell me, you missed the flight back.'
– 'I know what you're going to say.'

Listen attentively to start with and make obvious eye contact. Smile and nod in the right places but keep focused on the speaker's eyes. Maintain eye contact for longer than feels natural.

After a few moments, allow your gaze to wander to the speaker's mouth and study their teeth intently.

Fold your arms. Listen to your partner but interrupt them regularly to question, criticize or clarify what they've said:
'Why didn't you hire a bigger car?'
'Don't you like going abroad then?'
'That must have cost a fortune!'
'You should have booked it on the Internet'.

Listen for a few moments and then say 'Oh, you saying that has just reminded me ... '
Then proceed to change the subject completely and talk about something entirely irrelevant. Don't allow your partner to return to their story.

Listen attentively, smile and make suitable eye contact. From time to time, make comments or ask questions that clearly show you haven't been listening. E.g. 'Did you like the food in Italy then?' (When the story is about a vacation in France).

Notes for OHT 3.2

Adopt supportive body language

- Lean discretely towards the speaker.
- Maintain a comfortable level of eye contact.
- Nod, smile, raise eyebrows as appropriate.
- Mirror facial expressions.

Take the speaker seriously

- Don't pre-judge or jump to conclusions.
- Try to understand where they are coming from.
- Leave your prejudices to one side.

Concentrate attention on the speaker

- Limit possible distractions and interruptions from others (if impossible it may be better to suggest a later and quieter time to talk properly – but don't forget).
- Write down key words to keep attention fixed.
- Don't allow yourself to become focused instead on their accent or physical appearance.

Paraphrase facts and feelings

- Repeat message back to show you've heard, e.g. 'He didn't turn up?'
- Make verbal responses such as 'mm', 'I see' or 'Really?'
- Acknowledge emotions as in, 'I can see why you're so upset' or 'No wonder you are so excited'.

Allow the speaker to have their say

- Don't interrupt or butt in.
- Angry speakers, in particular, need to let off steam without interruption.
- Avoid the temptation to give advice unless asked.

Accept silences

- No matter how uncomfortable it may feel, silences can be an important part of coming to terms with a difficult issue. Give the speaker thinking time.

Think about what is being said

- Even if the subject in question bores you, look for something interesting in what is being said.
- Work out the key points.
- Keep up with what the speaker is saying rather than reflect back.

Listen between the lines

- Be aware of the speaker's body language and tone of voice.

GOOD LISTENING SKILLS

- Adopt supportive body language

- Take the speaker seriously

- Concentrate attention on the speaker

- Paraphrase facts and feelings

- Allow the speaker to have their say

- Accept silences

- Think about what is being said

- Listen between the lines

▶ ACTIVITY 3.3: REHEARSING GOOD LISTENING SKILLS

Ask participants to think about a significant event in their lives that they would be willing to share with a good listening partner (for example, a birth, move, new job, accident, a personal achievement or difficulty).

Each partner should spend five minutes telling their partner about their experience.

The listener should make every attempt to employ the good listening skills as previously discussed and avoid the inhibitors.

After each listening activity, the speaker should feed back in private to the listener on his/her listening behaviour.

TEAM POST-SESSION PLAN

UNIT 3: ARE WE A LISTENING TEAM?

How much support do we provide for one another? Are there any ways in which this level of support could be improved?

1.

2.

3.

Actions to be taken:

INDIVIDUAL POST-SESSION PLAN

UNIT 3: ARE WE A LISTENING TEAM?

Task for the next session

REFLECTIVE LOG

UNIT 3: ARE WE A LISTENING TEAM?

What aspects of your listening behaviour do you need to improve?

Think of an individual with whom you sometimes find it difficult to relate (family member/colleague/pupil). How might this session help you to enhance that relationship?

What Can We Do to Raise Pupil Self-Esteem?

UNIT OBJECTIVES

This unit will examine the concept of self-esteem and explore strategies for raising pupil self-esteem in school.

The objectives of the unit are:

- to clarify what we mean by self-esteem
- to illustrate the relationship between self-esteem, motivation and classroom behaviour
- to identify characteristics of high and low self-esteem
- to demonstrate approaches and strategies for enhancing self-esteem.

The session activities are designed to support the teaching assistant to:

- gain some insight into theories of self
- understand how self-esteem impact on learner behaviour
- recognize characteristics of high and low self-esteem
- develop strategies and approaches that may enhance pupil self-esteem.

PRIOR TO THE SESSION

Teaching assistants should complete the pre-session task sheet and bring it with them to the session.

SESSION MATERIALS AND AUDIO/VISUAL AIDS

- Overhead projector.
- Flip chart and pens.
- Pre-session task sheet (one copy for each).

UNIT 4 RESOURCES

Pre-session task
OHT 4.1: Pupils with high self-esteem
OHT 4.2: Pupils with low self-esteem
Activity 4.1: What is self-esteem?
Activity 4.2: What does self-esteem look like?
Team post-session plan
Individual post-session plan
Reflective log

NOTES FOR SENCO/TRAINER: WHAT CAN WE DO TO RAISE PUPIL SELF-ESTEEM?

Some knowledge and understanding of the concept of self-esteem and its relationship to learning and behaviour is of paramount importance to all those who work directly with pupils in schools. We know, from our own experience, that when we feel good about ourselves and confident in our abilities, we are more likely to feel secure in new learning situations. Conversely, when we feel inadequate, unimportant or unsure of our ability, our performance is likely to suffer as a result. The same is true for pupils.

In this unit, team members will learn that self-esteem:

- can fluctuate depending on the circumstance
- can be shaped through the reactions and responses of other people
- can be enhanced or damaged in a single event
- is reflected in the quality of interpersonal relationships
- is reflected in social behaviour
- affects motivation and achievement.

It is worth emphasizing that socializing and learning are risky businesses because the fear of rejection or failure is always present. As adults, we have some measure of control over the learning situations we place ourselves in. We may choose to take up salsa dancing, Japanese, or hang-gliding, but can usually feel safe in the knowledge that we can opt out if the going gets tough. Being the only person who has yet to master the skill is not a comfortable position to find yourself in. Similarly, if you find yourself at a party with no one to talk to, you can usually choose to leave early and have an early night instead. In such situations our self-esteem may well take a temporary dive, and if the same thing happens on a regular basis, then we might stop believing in our abilities altogether. For pupils in school, there is rarely the option to withdraw from stressful learning and social situations in a dignified way, and those who find it hardest to access the curriculum or interact positively with peers may face these challenges on a daily basis. Defence mechanisms such as wasting time, feigning illness, playing the clown,

PRE-SESSION TASK

a) I felt so proud of myself when

....

because ....

....

....

b) I felt really confident about

....

because ....

....

....

c) I felt really out of my depth when

....

d) I dread it when I have to

....

because ....

....

....

absconding and acting-out can all provide the necessary reprieve that will protect them from further humiliation and discomfort. In other words, low self-esteem can help to explain some of the challenging behaviours we are dealing with in school.

In order to identify low self-esteem in pupils, we need to be aware of the characteristics that are associated with it. Activity 4.2 is designed to demonstrate that we sometimes misinterpret and overlook what is sometimes referred to as 'false high esteem'. This is where individuals may adopt bravado strategies to disguise their insecurity. There are approaches and strategies that can help to enhance pupil self-esteem, some of which are suggested later in the unit. There will be other ideas that team members can bring to the discussion.

FURTHER READING

Barrow, G., Bradshaw, E. and Newton, T. (2001) *Improving Behaviour and Raising Self-Esteem in the Classroom*. London: David Fulton.

Fox, G. (2001) *Supporting Children with Behaviour Difficulties: A Guide for Assistants in Schools*. London: David Fulton.

STRUCTURE OF THE SESSION

A suggested structure is as follows.

Use the introductory notes to set this unit of work in context. Explain that the purpose of the pre-session task is to illustrate how high and low self-esteem can impact on our behaviour and willingness to learn or participate in social situations. In other words, nothing breeds success like success and the same is true for failure.

▶ ACTIVITY 4.1: WHAT IS SELF-ESTEEM?

Write the following questions on a flip chart:

- Who am I?
- What am I like?
- What would I wish to be like?

Ask the team members to write these down and add one or two sentences in response to each. While they do this, write the headings 'Self-concept', 'Self-image' and 'Ideal self' on the next three sheets of flip-chart paper. Taking each question in turn, ask for feedback and record some of the themes under each heading. So, for example, in answer to the first question the themes you record might include: name, marital status, parental status, ethnicity, gender, occupation, religion, age. These are indicators of self-concept.

The second question explores self-image and responses may include personal qualities, talents, weaknesses, appearance, personality traits, etc. When they are feeding back, ask the participants 'How do you *know* you are like that?' This is to elicit from them the fact that other people shape our self-image. We constantly compare and rank ourselves against others. The thoughts we have about ourselves are those that others have reflected back to us.

The responses to the third question could be similar to those in either of the first two, and reveal the 'ideal self'. Where do we get these 'ideal' images from? Discuss the impact of media images, role models, peer pressure, etc. It is perfectly normal for there to be a mismatch between our self-image and our ideal self. This is what aspirations are.

Where individuals accept that discrepancy and feel comfortable with who they are, then self-esteem is said to be high. If, on the other hand, individuals become fixated with achieving their ideal self, their self-image will be rejected and this is an indicator of low self-esteem and can lead to mental health problems.

▶ ACTIVITY 4.2: WHAT DOES SELF-ESTEEM LOOK LIKE?

Divide the team into two or more groups. Ideally, each group should contain a minimum of two and a maximum of five members. Give each group a large sheet of paper and felt-tip markers. Their task is to draw a picture of a child with either high or low self-esteem (depending on how you allocate this). Ensure that you commission some of each type, and if there is an odd number of groups, make the extra one a 'high' self-esteem image. Ask the groups to nominate one person to draw, but everyone should contribute ideas and the images should be annotated with thought and speech bubbles. Give the groups a time limit and then collect the images and put them to one side until later.

Notes for OHT 4.1

PUPILS WITH HIGH SELF-ESTEEM

In order to help raise pupil self-esteem we need to be able to identify it. OHT 4.1 offers some of the characteristics associated with *high* self-esteem. The following points could be added/emphasized:

- High esteem is not dependent on high ability. Some very able pupils may have low self-esteem and vice versa.
- Pupils with high self-esteem are able to recognize their strengths as well as their weaknesses.
- Pupils with high self-esteem recognize other people's strengths.
- They feel comfortable with who they are.
- They are happy to work with pupils outside of their friendship group.
- They like a challenge but 'bounce back' if things don't go according to plan.
- They interact well with adults in school but prefer the company of peers.
- They tend to display what psychologists call 'internal locus of control'. This means, they believe that they have some control over what happens to them. They can admit their mistakes and acknowledge their efforts rather than blame outside factors or put their success down to good fortune.
- Think of colleagues, friends, relatives or acquaintances who exhibit these characteristics and reflect upon your own position.

Divide the team into pairs or small groups of colleagues who share knowledge of the same pupils. Ask each pair or group to discuss and consider the pupils they work with. Can they identify certain pupils in the school who exhibit these characteristics of high self-esteem.

PUPILS WITH
HIGH SELF-ESTEEM

Achieve well
in relation to
their abilities

Are confident
in social
situations

Display natural
curiosity and will
embrace and relish
new challenges

Relate well
to adults
and peers

Present
fewer
behavioural
problems

PUPILS WITH LOW SELF-ESTEEM

OHT 4.2 provides some characteristics of *low* self-esteem. The following points can be used to expand upon this:

- Refer back to the point about learning being a risky business. There is a well-known saying: 'With no attempt there can be no failure. With no failure, no humiliation.' (William James, 1890). Pupils with low self-esteem tend to rely heavily on teaching assistants and/or peers because they lack confidence in their own abilities.

- Pupils with low self-esteem find it difficult to relate to and trust other people. They may hang around on the fringes of social groups or rely on the company of trusted adults. They may use manipulative methods such as lying or causing friction between others in an attempt to win friendship.

- Low self-esteem is associated with 'External Locus of Control'. In other words, these pupils will tend to blame other people and external factors for things that happen. They find it as difficult to admit that they are in the wrong as they do to accept compliments.

- A child that grows up receiving negative messages about themselves, will eventually come to believe those messages. Messages can be communicated overtly, for example, in name-calling or the use of labelling such as lazy, naughty, rude, etc. More subtle but equally powerful messages are communicated through actions such as exclusion from social events, placement in ability groups, etc.

- By criticizing other people and making 'put downs', the pupil with low self-esteem is protecting his/her ego.

- Boasting and showing-off are behavioural characteristics that we often associate with self-confidence. This is a false assumption. Pupils that have the need to try and impress others in this way are presenting what some psychologists refer to as 'false' or 'phoney' self-esteem.

- Think of colleagues, friends, relatives or acquaintances who display these characteristics and reflect upon your own position.

In the same working pairs or groups, consider and identify pupils that exhibit the characteristics of low self-esteem and false self-esteem. Now return to the drawings that were produced in Activity 4.2. Pin them up or hold each one up in turn for the group to see. Discuss the features of each. How closely do these match the characteristics shown in OHT 4.1 and 4.2? In our experience there are usually examples of 'false' esteem in the 'high' esteem pictures. This simply confirms that we sometimes misinterpret pupil behaviour and overlook signs of low self-esteem.

PUPILS WITH LOW SELF-ESTEEM

Appear apathetic in learning situations

Lack confidence in their relationships. Seek reassurance about whether or not they are liked

Are hesitant in new situations and may be reluctant to assume responsibility

Blame others for failure. Are hypercritical and quick to identify others' faults

Appear to be uncomfortable with praise. Make self-disparaging remarks

Boast and show-off to be the centre of attention

WHAT CAN WE DO TO RAISE PUPIL SELF-ESTEEM?

APPROACHES AND STRATEGIES

An American psychologist, Eric Berne, described the concept of psychological strokes. According to this theory, units of positive recognition make us feel valued, appreciated, included and, ultimately, better about ourselves. A unit of unconditional positive recognition can be anything from a smile from a stranger in the street, a thank you from our partner, a kind word, a mention in the school newsletter, an offer of or request for help, a compliment, an invitation, a knowing wink or even a raise in salary! Each of these actions can have the effect of making us feel acknowledged and valued as a human being.

It is important to remind ourselves that some children go through their lives at home and school hearing predominantly negative messages about themselves and receiving few psychological strokes. Our knowledge and experience of behaviour management tells us that pupils who receive little in the way of positive praise and attention will seek alternative ways of getting noticed. The implication here, then, is that psychological strokes or unconditional, positive recognition may help to enhance the self-esteem of pupils. By adopting a positive style of behaviour management (see Unit 7) and an assertive approach (see Unit 6) we can help to raise the self-esteem of all pupils. Don't forget that pupils with low self-esteem may deflect and appear to reject positive units of recognition, but this doesn't mean we should give up on the psychological strokes. These are the pupils that need them most! To be effective, psychological strokes need to be sincere. An over-effusive or gushing approach will be perceived as false. Pupils with low self-esteem often find it easier to accept subtle and less public recognition.

Ask the group to brainstorm specific interventions and strategies that are currently used in school to enhance pupil self-esteem. Record these on a flip chart. (For example: circle time, pupil of the week, mentoring, use of responsibilities and privileges, friendship tree, circle of friends, etc.) To what extent do these strategies benefit (a) all pupils? and (b) individual pupils with low self-esteem?

Consider how this aspect could be further developed.

TEAM POST-SESSION PLAN

UNIT 4: WHAT CAN WE DO TO RAISE PUPIL SELF-ESTEEM?

What aspects of improving pupil self-esteem do we need to work on as a whole team?

1.

2.

3.

Actions to be taken:

INDIVIDUAL POST-SESSION PLAN

UNIT 4: WHAT CAN WE DO TO RAISE PUPIL SELF-ESTEEM?

Task for the next session

REFLECTIVE LOG

UNIT 4: WHAT CAN WE DO TO RAISE PUPIL SELF-ESTEEM?

What have you learned about yourself and your own level of self-esteem?

How do you intend to help raise the self-esteem of pupils you support?

Do We Promote Emotional Literacy?

UNIT OBJECTIVES

Emotional literacy is seen as the ability to recognize, understand, handle and express emotions appropriately. This unit outlines the link between learning, behaviour and emotional literacy, and explores the approaches that can be taken to promote emotional literacy in the classroom.

The objectives of the unit are:

- to support teaching assistants to develop the personal and professional skills to understand and manage emotions and to communicate effectively
- to consider tasks and activities that nurture emotional literacy skills in the classroom
- to emphasize how secure school environments can help promote emotional well-being.

The session activities are designed to support the teaching assistant to:

- understand the importance of the link between learning, behaviour and emotional literacy
- reflect upon their own emotional responses to pupil behaviour
- consider why some children experience and exhibit emotional difficulties
- plan and respond appropriately to pupils' emotional understanding and development.

PRIOR TO THE SESSION

Ask the team to consider details of:

- an interaction they have had with a pupil that has left them feeling very positive
- an interaction they have had with a pupil that has left them feeling less than positive.

SESSION MATERIALS AND AUDIO/VISUAL AIDS

- Overhead projector.
- Flip-chart sheets and pens.

UNIT 5 RESOURCES

OHT 5.1: What is emotional literacy?
OHT 5.2: How am I feeling?
OHT 5.3: Ways in which teaching assistants can support emotional literacy
ACTIVITY 5.1: An emotional vocabulary
ACTIVITY 5.2: I feel.........when..........
ACTIVITY 5.3: Feeling good.........feeling not so good
Team post-session plan
Individual post-session plan
Reflective log

NOTES FOR SENCO/TRAINER: DO WE PROMOTE EMOTIONAL LITERACY?

Children who experience behavioural difficulties may also have problems in expressing, managing and dealing with their emotions appropriately. These problems may be displayed in a number of ways: at one end of the spectrum, sudden outbursts of anger and frustration; and, at the other, periods of intense introspection and withdrawal. For some children, feelings of emotional hurt may be overwhelming and confusing, contributing significantly to their self-esteem (see UNIT 3) and negatively affecting relationships both with peers and adults.

In the classroom, children exhibiting emotional difficulties may appear to be reluctant to try new areas of work, lack self-confidence in their own abilities and find it difficult to make or sustain friendships. Often such emotionally vulnerable children will find it difficult to express their feelings appropriately or to recognize, interpret or respond to the feelings of others around them.

They may quickly lose their temper, hit or kick out at peers, continually quarrel, seek attention and appear insensitive to the feelings of others. They may be oversensitive to correction or criticism, be unable to accept praise and find difficulty in accepting help and support. Often the child's actions and responses will form an observable pattern of behaviour that may be repeated on a regular basis in specific contexts and situations.

The child may not be aware that they are repeating these patterns of behaviour or may not yet have learnt alternative and more appropriate ways of expressing and managing their emotions. Some children may not be able to explain why they are afraid, unhappy or angry and so express it through their behaviour. Emotional difficulties can become a significant barrier to learning.

There may be underlying causal factors that impact on a child's life experiences and contribute to their feelings of social competency, emotional well-being and self-worth. These include:

- **Social and environmental factors**
  i.e. family breakdown; family health and psychiatric problems; parenting styles, quality of child care; poverty; poor housing; social pressures; abuse and violence in the home
- **Psychological factors**
  i.e. individual differences, perceptions and personality influenced by early experiences; sense of self; trauma; grief and loss; stress; mental health problems
- **Medical and biological factors**
  i.e. sensory difficulties; specific disabilities; neurological conditions; delayed development
- **School based factors**
  i.e. previous negative experiences of school; unrecognized special educational needs; poor attendance.

These factors are identified as contributing to:
- mental health difficulties
- the lessening of a child's resilience to risk and uncertainty
- low self-esteem
- lack of confidence in their ability to deal with change and adaptation
- uncertainty and confusion in forming social relationships
- difficulties in understanding their own feelings and the feelings of others
- confusion as to the consequences of their own actions and the actions of others
- feelings of isolation and rejection.

Positive school environments can mitigate the effects of stress and adversity. For some children, school may be the only stable and structured influence in their lives, and may provide a safe and secure environment in which they can be supported and where trusted adults help them to understand and control their emotional responses. In times of stress and crisis, children will often turn for support to a member of staff with whom they feel they have a trusting and safe relationship.

WHY IS EMOTIONAL LITERACY IMPORTANT?

Emotions impact on every area of our everyday life – in matters related to our mental health, in the way we form and maintain relationships, in the way we behave and in the way we learn. Emotional literacy is a term that encompasses a range of skills and attributes related to:

- how we identify, understand and clarify our own feelings
- how we express and manage feelings appropriately
- how we recognize and respond to others' feelings
- how we form and maintain relationships

- how we deal successfully with conflict
- how we learn new ways of behaving.

It is most likely that children who are emotionally competent by managing their own feelings well, and who recognize and respond effectively to the feelings of others, will feel confident and secure in their learning. Learning is an emotional experience that involves the child in risk-taking – being able to tackle new areas of work, new experiences and new relationships with confidence in their own abilities to succeed.

THE EMOTIONALLY LITERATE SCHOOL

Education is concerned with the development of the whole person – physical, intellectual and *emotional* aspects. Good practice indicates that successful and effective schools are characterized by an ethos which promotes emotional competency as an essential component of the learning process. Emotionally literate schools will promote a vision of themselves as inclusive learning communities. This will be apparent in the supportive structures of the school, the content and delivery of the curriculum, the range of teaching approaches employed and the focus put upon nurturing positive relationships in the interactions between all members of the school community.

Opportunities will be available across the curriculum for pupils to:

- learn how to identify and understand their feelings
- learn how to express their feelings appropriately
- learn how to recognize the feelings of others
- rehearse ways of behaving and managing feelings in new or difficult situations.

CLASSROOM APPROACHES

Evaluating your own personal style in the classroom is a good first step to developing a programme of emotional literacy for your pupils. Knowing when (and why) you feel at your best in the classroom will give you an insight into the strategies you might employ at the times when you feel tired, emotionally exhausted or stressed. Also, analysing and identifying the particular classroom situations or interactions that have frustrated you in the past will enable you to think of alternative ways you might counter them in the future.

Be aware of your own feelings and responses when a pupil exhibits difficult behaviour in the classroom. In interactions with pupils who present as emotionally charged or vulnerable ask the questions:

- *Am I aware of the child's emotion and cause of it?*
- *Am I actively listening and acknowledging the child's feelings?*

Each lesson may provide general opportunities to engage pupils in emotional learning:

- by sharing thoughts and feelings about the subject matter of the lesson
- by encouraging pupils to talk about what they have learnt and their feelings about this

- by enabling pupils to give praise, positive feedback and encouragement to other pupils

One-to-one support in lessons with pupils with emotional and behavioural difficulties can help the pupil to develop alternative strategies and build up skills on a step-by-step basis. Forming a trusting and close relationship with an adult who shows positive regard, who is interested in the pupil's welfare and concerns, will inevitably bolster the pupil's self-esteem and confidence. Engaging the pupil in discussing how he/she is feeling or how his/her feelings lead to conflict or affect others can effectively be approached through individual activities and games constructed around issues and needs of the pupil. Although a child's emotional development is not necessarily a linear process, to enable him/her to use *an emotional vocabulary* (to recognize and name emotions) is an essential prerequisite to developing an understanding of one's own inner feelings. Children may not be able to explain why they are afraid, unhappy or angry and so express it through their behaviour. Learning an emotional vocabulary can be a starting point for work towards self-reflection.

Circle time and group work can provide structured, positive and safe formats for pupils to explore their feelings, to develop their confidence, to try out new responses, to discuss concerns and to develop their emotional competency. A range of games, problem-solving activities and art and drama work can be introduced to discuss and develop understanding of a range of issues including bullying/victim, fairness/unfairness, inclusion/exclusion and to give opportunities to pupils to:

- learn the vocabulary of feelings
- talk about how they feel about specific events
- discuss relationships, conflicts and dilemmas
- explore their emotional responses to given situations
- understand and appreciate other people's feelings.

FURTHER READING:

Mosely, J. (1996) *Quality Circle Time.* Wisbech: LDA.

Sharp, P. (2001) *Nurturing Emotional Literacy: A Practical Guide for Teachers, Parents and Those in the Caring Professions.* London: David Fulton.

STRUCTURE OF THE SESSION

A suggested structure is as follows.

Notes for OHT 5.1

WHAT IS EMOTIONAL LITERACY?

Introduce the session by asking the team how they are feeling as they have arrived for the session. There is likely to be a range of responses depending on levels of energy, unresolved issues prior to the session, etc. Ask the team when was the last time – during the day, during the week – when they were last asked how they were feeling. Introduce the topic using OHT 5.1.

WHAT IS EMOTIONAL LITERACY?

The ability to recognize, understand, handle and appropriately express emotions –

- how we identify, understand and clarify our own feelings

- how we express and manage feelings appropriately

- how we recognize and respond to others' feelings

- how we form and maintain relationships

- how we deal successfully with conflict

- how we learn new ways of behaving

▶ ACTIVITY 5.1: AN EMOTIONAL VOCABULARY

In this activity, pairs/small groups are asked to write on a flip-chart sheet all the words they can think of that are EMOTION words. Ask the pairs/small groups to display their sheet and discuss. Use the flip chart to add further words that are suggested by the discussion.

Use OHT 5.2 to check any words if not suggested.

Notes for OHT 5.2

HOW AM I FEELING?

OHT 5.2 identifies some of the key emotion words we use in our everyday interactions to describe how we feel. Discuss with the team the meanings for the different words we use and ask for examples of the situations in which we might use them.

HOW AM I FEELING?

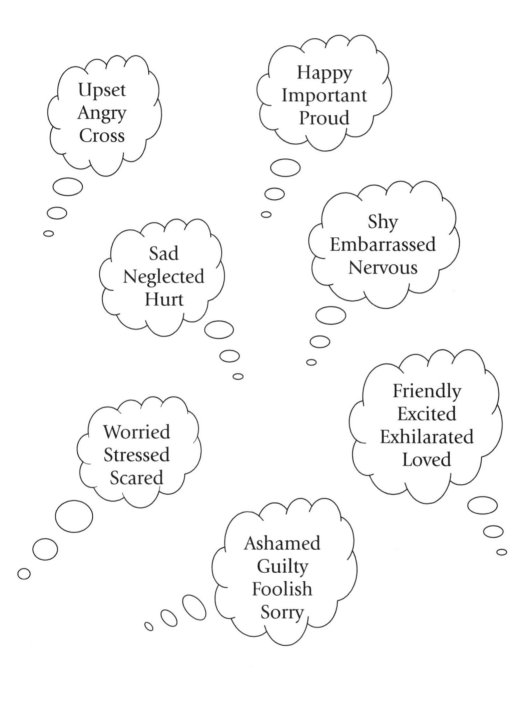

▶ ACTIVITY 5.2: I FEEL.........WHEN........

Ask the individual team members to complete the statements I FEEL.........WHEN..........
When complete ask if they would like to share with a partner.

Discuss with the whole team how they felt about the activity.

1. I feel angry when . . . .

2. I feel happy when . . . .

3. I feel sad when . . . .

4. I feel nervous when . . . .

5. I feel surprised when . . . .

6. I feel exhilarated when . . . .

7. I feel guilty when . . . .

8. I feel hurt when . . . .

9. I feel excited . . . .

10. I feel worried when . . . .

▶ ACTIVITY 5.3: FEELING GOOD...
...FEELING NOT SO GOOD

Using Activity Sheets 3a and 3b individual members of the
team are asked to complete details of:

■ an interaction they have had with a pupil that has left
   them feeling very positive
■ an interaction they have had with a pupil that has left
   them feeling less than positive.

Give time after completion to share with a partner. Ask
members of the team if one or two would share theirs with
the whole group. Ask for feedback.

Detail an interaction that you have had recently with a pupil that has left you feeling very positive.

What happened?

What made you feel good about this?

Detail an interaction that you have had recently with a pupil which has left you feeling less than positive.

What happened?

What made you feel less than positive about this?

How could you have improved the outcome?

Notes for OHT 5.3

WAYS IN WHICH TEACHING ASSISTANTS CAN SUPPORT EMOTIONAL LITERACY

OHT 5.3 identifies some of the areas of work in which the team demonstrates its contribution to emotional literacy.

Ask the team to add other aspects of their work to those displayed on the OHT. Collate responses on the flip chart and pin it up.

WAYS IN WHICH TEACHING ASSISTANTS CAN SUPPORT EMOTIONAL LITERACY

- Showing positive regard

- Being a welcoming and listening ear

- Showing real interest and concern

- By remaining calm

- By acknowledging the child's feelings

- By helping them to express how they feel

TEAM POST-SESSION PLAN

UNIT 5: DO WE PROMOTE EMOTIONAL LITERACY?

In what ways can we further promote emotional literacy as a team?

1.

2.

3.

Actions to be taken:

INDIVIDUAL POST-SESSION PLAN

UNIT 5: DO WE PROMOTE EMOTIONAL LITERACY?

Task for the next session

REFLECTIVE LOG

UNIT 5: DO WE PROMOTE EMOTIONAL LITERACY?

How does your knowledge and understanding of emotional literacy help you in your teaching assistant role?

What implications might it have for future practice?

Raising our Confidence in Managing Behaviour

UNIT OBJECTIVES

This unit is designed to help team members feel more empowered in both their personal and professional lives through enhanced self-awareness and the development of assertion skills.

The objectives of the unit are:

- to clarify what is meant by assertive behaviour
- to introduce the basic techniques of assertiveness
- to provide opportunities for practising assertive communication
- to recognise the importance of non-verbal communication.

The session activities are designed to support the teaching assistant to:

- understand the difference between passive, aggressive, manipulative and assertive behaviour
- be able to express feelings and personal needs more effectively
- rehearse techniques of assertion
- feel more confident and assertive in their dealings with pupil behaviour.

PRIOR TO THE SESSION

Teaching assistants should be given a copy of the AQ quiz to complete in private. These should then be brought to the session.

SESSION MATERIALS AND AUDIO/VISUAL AIDS:

- Overhead projector.
- Flip chart and pen.
- AQ quiz sheet (one copy per person).

UNIT 6 RESOURCES

AQ quiz sheet
OHT 6.1: Submissive behaviour
OHT 6.2: Aggressive behaviour
OHT 6.3: Manipulative behaviour
OHT 6.4: Assertive behaviour
OHT 6.5: Assertiveness
OHT 6.6: Making a complaint/offering critical feedback
Activity 6.1: AQ quiz
Activity 6.2: Self-review
Activity 6.3: Voice tone and body language
Activity 6.4: Practising the broken record
Activity 6.5: Practise giving critical feedback
Team post-session plan
Individual post-session plan
Reflective log

NOTES FOR SENCO/TRAINER

Few professionals would claim to be experts in behaviour management. At some time or another, all teachers and teaching assistants will have experienced the emotions of anxiety, frustration, anger and uncertainty when faced with challenging pupil behaviour. It is important to begin this unit of work by reiterating this point so that colleagues do not feel inadequate or singled out in any way. Assertiveness training can help to enhance confidence, improve communication skills and empower individuals in their personal and professional lives. This unit provides a brief introduction to assertive behaviour techniques.

The AQ (assertiveness quotient) quiz provides a good starting point for the session as it encourages some light-hearted, self-reflection. Ideally, this should be distributed prior to the session, but it could be used as an introductory activity. Some individuals may notice a pattern in their responses while others may see a contrast in their home and school responses. It should be pointed out, however, that behaviour is always contextual rather than fixed and, even if we show a tendency towards a behaviour type, it doesn't have to mean we cannot change it. Self-awareness is the first step. The distinction between the following behaviour patterns is also introduced through the quiz:

- submissive
- aggressive
- manipulative
- assertive.

The first three types are all regarded as non-assertive (although many people wrongly confuse aggressive responses with assertive ones). The activities in this unit provide

AQ Quiz

Please answer yes or no to the following questions

AT HOME

1. Do you often feel taken for granted by your partner and/or children?
2. Do you shout (or swear) a lot because that's the only way to get heard?
3. Do you insist that your partner/housemate does their fair share of the housework?
4. Do you ever pretend to make a start on a job you wanted someone else to do, in the hope that they'll notice and take over?

AT SCHOOL

1. Do you sometimes turn a blind eye to misbehaviour because the pupils would probably ignore you anyway?
2. Have you ever felt angry or frustrated enough to tell a pupil that he/she is stupid/pathetic/a waste of space?
3. Would you feel able to speak out in a staff meeting if you felt someone was being treated unfairly?
4. Do you make up excuses to avoid playground duty/working with a particular pupil or teacher?

THE OUTSIDE WORLD

1. Do you find it hard to accept a compliment about your appearance or achievements?
2. Do you tell double-glazing telesales people where to go?
3. Could you ask an important visitor to refrain from smoking in your home?
4. If someone pushes in front of you, do you say (in a loud voice) to your child/friend 'Oh charming! What's the point in having a queue?'

opportunities for team members to reflect upon their own styles of behaviour and should help them to identify areas of their lives in which they might benefit from developing more assertive responses. OHT 6.5 defines what is meant by assertiveness.

Activity 6.3 encourages participants to be more aware of their body language and non-verbal communication. Assertive behaviour is more than just a set of verbal scripts. Non-verbal behaviour can reveal an individual's true feelings and where there is a confusing mismatch between verbal and non-verbal messages, and this is known as 'leakage'.

Participants have the opportunity to practise a number of assertion skills to help them interact more effectively at home and school. The majority of these activities are conducted in pairs. It is advisable to encourage different pairings for some activities so that participants benefit from a range of experiences.

The session finishes with an activity in which team members are asked to consider their personal strengths. Refer back to OHT 6.5 to remind colleagues about the characteristics of assertive behaviour. In order to interact in a mutually respective way, individuals need to develop self-respect. However, social and cultural constraints often make it difficult for us to celebrate our strengths and accept compliments assertively. There is also an opportunity to reflect upon the strengths of the team/school as well as on the individual level.

FURTHER READING

Mosley, J. and Gillibrand, E. (2001) *She Who Dares Wins.* Trowbridge: Positive Press.

STRUCTURE OF THE SESSION

A suggested structure is as follows.

> ▶ ACTIVITY 6.1: AQ QUIZ
>
> In pairs, or groups of three, team members go through the questions in the quiz that was distributed before the session and share their responses. Allow plenty of time for discussion as this activity is good for sharing common experiences and developing self-awareness. Do not ask for whole-group feedback at this stage. Instead, circulate around the groups/pairs and encourage discussion where required.

Notes for OHT 6.1–6.4

ELEMENTS OF THE WHOLE-SCHOOL BEHAVIOUR POLICY

Next, go through OHTs 6.1–6.4. These illustrate the kinds of thoughts and attitudes associated with each behaviour type reflected in the quiz. Ask the team members if they recognize their own response patterns. Refer them back to their quiz responses. Questions numbered (1) reflect submissive behaviour, (2) aggressive behaviour, (3) assertive behaviour and (4) manipulative behaviour.

SUBMISSIVE BEHAVIOUR

I don't like to make a fuss!

Can you ask her for me?

Oh go on then, you've talked me
into it!

Sorry, it's my fault!
(When it clearly isn't)

AGGRESSIVE BEHAVIOUR

I'm not letting him get one over
on me!

I don't care what people think, I just
speak my mind!

He keeps well out of my way
these days!

I'm not listening to your
pathetic excuse!

MANIPULATIVE BEHAVIOUR

It's OK, I'll do it, even though it means missing
my lunch again!

I wouldn't touch that display! Mrs Smith might
see you. Then you'll be for it!

Oh go on, do it for me! I'll get into trouble
with Mr Betts if you don't finish it this lesson.

I'm sure someone told me the meeting had
been cancelled!
(When you simply forgot to go)

96

ASSERTIVE BEHAVIOUR

I'm afraid I can't stay late this evening because I have another commitment, but I could come in earlier tomorrow.

Can we talk about that misunderstanding last lesson?

I was really impressed with the way you handled that.

I felt quite humiliated when you spoke to me that way in front of the pupils.

ASSERTIVENESS

The ability to express feelings, opinions and wishes in a clear, direct and honest way.

The ability to interact with others in a way that maintains mutual respect and dignity.

The ability to discuss, negotiate and compromise.

The ability to give and receive effective feedback.

The right to say 'yes' and 'no'.

▶ ACTIVITY 6.2: SELF-REVIEW

In pairs: Can you identify your principal style? Try to think of an example where you have acted in an aggressive, submissive or manipulative way. Discuss your reasons for adopting this approach.

▶ ACTIVITY 6.3: VOICE TONE AND BODY LANGUAGE

This can be done in small groups. Write three or four phrases or instructions on the flip chart. For example: 'Put that equipment back in the cupboard, it shouldn't be out', 'I need two volunteers to help with the chairs', 'Could you take my coffee cup back to the staff room please?' Group members take it in turns to say the phrases/instructions to the others, using a different style and tone (aggressive, manipulative, submissive, assertive) each time. At the end of the activity, ask the team what they noticed about body language associated with each type. You may need to repeat the activity or ask for one or two demonstrations (remember to ask assertively).

▪ USING THE BROKEN RECORD TECHNIQUE

The key aspects of this technique are calmness, persistency and the avoidance of side issues. The aim is to repeat your message until the other person eventually receives it. There is a need to keep focused and ignore any attempt that the other person makes to manipulate or dominate. Check out your own body language for signs of 'leakage'.

This technique can be useful when:

- a pupil refuses to follow a reasonable request
- someone is trying to persuade you to do something that you don't want to do.

Some useful scripts are:

- Perhaps you do think that but ... (repeat assertion).
- Yes I see that, but what I'm saying is ... (repeat assertion).
- I'm asking you to ... (repeat assertion).
- I don't think you are listening, I've said that ... (repeat assertion).
- That may be true but ... (repeat assertion).
- I know it's difficult but ... (repeat assertion).

These (and others may be suggested by the group) can be recorded on a flip chart for reference during the following activity.

▶ ACTIVITY 6.4: PRACTISING THE BROKEN RECORD

In pairs, discuss situations where you might use the broken record technique to convey your message more effectively. Try to think of one situation at home and one at school. Now role-play the interactions. The opposite partner should try to use a range of counter-arguments but should concede when they feel the broken record makes a continuation of the conversation uncomfortable.

■ DEALING WITH CRITICISM AND COMPLAINTS

Criticism often provokes a submissive, aggressive or manipulative response from us, and this is sometimes because of the way that the criticism is offered.

First, ask the group members to reflect on how they respond to criticism:

- Aggressively? By retaliating with hurtful or spiteful comments back.
- Submissively? By apologizing even if the criticism is unfounded?
- Manipulatively? By shifting the blame onto someone else?

Being on the receiving end of criticism is bound to evoke feelings of hurt, guilt, disappointment, embarrassment or annoyance. Bear this in mind when pupils react adversely when being corrected. The following techniques can also help individuals to deal assertively with criticism.

FOGGING

Try not to argue back as this gives the person more ammunition. Be non-defensive, accept the truth (or possible truth) in what is said and let the person know that you have heard them. For example:

Criticism: 'You're much too soft on him!'

Response: 'You could be right. I did give him an extra chance that time.'

NEGATIVE ENQUIRY

If the criticism seems unjust or too general, prompt the person to clarify and specify. For example:

Criticism: 'There was far too much noise coming from the hall, they must have been running riot.'

Response: 'The children were quite noisy but what makes you think they were running riot?'

Ask team members to think of a time when they found it difficult to *give* criticism or make a complaint. OHT 6.6 provides a helpful framework for structuring this feedback. Keep this OHT on the screen as a reference point during Activity 6.5.

> ► ACTIVITY 6.5: PRACTISE GIVING CRITICAL FEEDBACK
>
> In pairs, use the framework provided on OHT 6.6 to help plan and rehearse the making of a complaint or offer of critical feedback. Take it in turns to role-play each part and watch one another's body language. Real or hypothetical situations can be used as examples. The receiver of the complaint or criticism should also try to respond in an assertive way.

■ GIVING AND RECEIVING COMPLIMENTS

Social and cultural constraints sometimes make it difficult to receive compliments assertively. In short, we feel uncomfortable about being told good things about ourselves. The aggressive response may be to wonder what the person is after. The submissive response would be to deflect the credit elsewhere and the manipulative approach is to 'fish' for compliments.

Offering positive feedback is part of our work in schools but when was the last time we gave (or received) positive feedback to a colleague or family member? Discuss these points as a group and conclude the session by asking the team to reflect on their own personal strengths as well as those of the team. You could even end the session with a quick round (circle time fashion) where individuals each divulge a personal strength.

MAKING A COMPLAINT/OFFERING CRITICAL FEEDBACK

- Explain the situation

- Acknowledge the other person's feelings

- Outline your needs

- Outline the consequences

TEAM POST-SESSION PLAN

UNIT 6: RAISING OUR CONFIDENCE IN MANAGING BEHAVIOUR

How can we support one another more effectively in the management of pupil behaviour? (Remember to use your assertiveness skills to express your wants and needs.)

1.

2.

3.

Actions to be taken:

INDIVIDUAL POST-SESSION PLAN

UNIT 6: RAISING OUR CONFIDENCE IN MANAGING BEHAVIOUR

Task for the next session

REFLECTIVE LOG

UNIT 6: RAISING OUR CONFIDENCE IN MANAGING BEHAVIOUR

In which situations would you like to behave more assertively?

What assertiveness strategies will you try to incorporate into your practice?

Developing Strategies for Effective Behaviour Management

UNIT OBJECTIVES

This unit will explore a range of strategies and approaches for positive behaviour management.

The objectives of the unit are:

- to consider how the behaviour of staff impacts on pupil behaviour
- to compare and contrast different styles of behaviour management
- to demonstrate the need for planning in behaviour management
- to promote the use of positive verbal and non-verbal communication.

The session activities are designed to support the teaching assistant to:

- recognize and learn more about their own style of behaviour management
- be more conscious of the need for forward planning in behaviour management
- develop their communication skills
- learn techniques for diffusing conflict and arguments.

PRIOR TO THE SESSION

Teaching assistants should spend a week prior to the session observing and considering how pupil behaviour is managed in school. They should reflect on styles of interaction between adults and pupils, and identify strategies that appear to be effective in managing behaviour.

SESSION MATERIALS AND AUDIO/VISUAL AIDS

- Overhead projector.
- Flip chart and pen.
- Photocopied context cards for Activity 7.3 (optional).

UNIT 7 RESOURCES

OHT 7.1: Styles of behaviour management
OHT 7.2a: Would I know what to do if ... ? (Primary)
OHT 7.2b: Would I know what to do if ... ? (Secondary)
OHT 7.3: Developing positive language skills
OHT 7.4: Coaching appropriate behaviour
Activity 7.1: Styles of behaviour management
Activity 7.2: What's my style?
Activity 7.3: Role-play exercise – handling arguments
Team post-session plan
Individual post-session plan
Reflective log

NOTES FOR SENCO/TRAINER

It should be emphasized to the team that although there are tips and techniques they can learn to help them manage behaviour more effectively, there are no easy, quick-fix solutions. Effective behaviour management is hard work and will require a commitment on the part of team members to look carefully at aspects of their own behaviour, attitudes and communication style. They should understand that they may need to make some changes in terms of their own behaviour. By approaching this as a team, however, they can support one another and impact more effectively on the general ethos of the school.

This unit is designed to promote the benefits of positive and assertive behaviour management approaches such as those advocated by Rogers (1990), O'Brien (1998) and others. The key to positive behaviour management is the quality of interaction between staff and pupils. Team members will be encouraged to consider how they can develop their communication skills to encourage and coach more positive behaviour from pupils, as well as correct behaviour in a way that maintains relationships and protects pupil self-esteem. The session is introduced by encouraging team members to reflect upon their own experiences as pupils and the impact that adult behaviour has on pupils' achievement and emotional development. They will then consider aspects of their own style of behaviour management and begin to think about how they might improve the quality of their interactions with pupils. A positive and assertive style of behaviour management is promoted.

The unit also identifies the need for forward planning at both personal and team level. In other words, it is helpful to think in advance about how we might deal with certain situations. A sharing of experiences is a good starting point here and OHT 7.2 can be used as the basis for discussion around this. It is very important, however, to establish an atmosphere of trust in which colleagues feel comfortable about admitting their doubts or anxieties. This section may also uncover aspects of the Whole-School Behaviour Policy that might need further discussion or review.

Finally, the unit focuses on the development of positive communication skills. Although a number of verbal strategies are introduced here, it is important to include aspects of non-verbal behaviour in this section. Ask the team to consider, and be aware of, body language that might override the verbal message that they are trying to deliver. Several strategies for positive communication with pupils are offered in this section.

Reacting and responding to challenging behaviour is a stressful business. Over time, it can lower staff morale and batter confidence. This unit aims to show the team that a positive and proactive approach (supported by a clear behaviour policy) can enhance the standard of pupil behaviour, improve relationships and generate more smiling and less frowning in school.

FURTHER READING

O'Brien, T. (1998) *Promoting Positive Behaviour.* London: David Fulton.

Rogers, B. (1990) *You Know the Fair Rule.* Harlow: Longman.

Rogers, B. (1997) *Behaviour Management.* Australia: Scholastic.

STRUCTURE OF THE SESSION

A suggested structure is as follows.

Notes for OHT 7.1

OHT 7.1: STYLES OF BEHAVIOUR MANAGEMENT

Use OHT 7.1 to help consolidate the distinction between different styles of behaviour management. Emphasize that these styles are contextual rather than fixed characteristics. We are all human! What factors might trigger an aggressive or passive response from us when faced with challenging behaviour? Finally, refer back to the 'admirable' qualities that you listed on the flip chart to illustrate why we should aspire to the assertive style of behaviour management

■ PLANNING AHEAD

In order to help us respond assertively to challenging behaviour (remember: calmly, consistently and confidently) it is important to plan ahead. This needs to be done on a team/staff basis as well as on a personal level. Members of staff regularly plan aspects of the curriculum together but they rarely plan for behaviour management in this systematic way. To introduce the need for a behaviour management plan use OHT 7.2a (more suitable for primary) or OHT 7.2b (more suitable for secondary) to initiate this process and encourage dialogue. The different responses that team members give may highlight areas for development and encourage further discussion about the school's behaviour policy. Also, use this opportunity to introduce the concept of least to most intrusive intervention (Rogers, 1990). This can be explained as a hierarchy of steps or responses that can help to prevent us from overreacting in certain situations or running out of options when dealing with challenging behaviour. Finally, this is a good opportunity to emphasize that, like any other skill, effective behaviour management can be learned, developed and refined through practice and commitment.

▶ ACTIVITY 7.1: STYLES OF BEHAVIOUR MANAGEMENT

Ask the team to think back to when they were pupils at school. In pairs or small groups, discuss and share some personal experiences of the following:

■ a teacher that made me feel frightened or anxious and why

■ a teacher that I disliked and why

■ a teacher that found it difficult to maintain discipline.

Feedback some experiences to the whole group. Emphasize that teacher behaviour can have a lasting impact on individuals. What effect might these adult styles have on a pupil's (a) achievement and (b) enjoyment of a subject? Next, ask the team to think about a teacher that they particularly admired and respected. Write down five or six qualities or characteristics that describe their style of pupil behaviour management. Record ideas on a flip chart.

▶ ACTIVITY 7.2: WHAT'S MY STYLE?

In pairs, can you identify your principal style of behaviour management? Now think of an incident in which you acted in an aggressive or passive way. How did you feel afterwards? How do you think the pupil(s) involved felt afterwards? Discuss how this might have been dealt with in a more assertive manner.

STYLES OF
BEHAVIOUR MANAGEMENT

Aggressive

Hostile, authoritarian, rigid, domineering, controlling

Passive

Insecure, unsure, inconsistent, helpless, disorganized

Assertive

Positive, calm, confident, decisive, consistent, fair

WOULD I KNOW WHAT TO DO IF … ?

A young autistic child was biting her own hand really hard?

A child refused to come out from under the table?

A pupil ran away from the playground and into the street?

A young pupil kept trying to climb onto my lap and hug me tightly round the neck?

A very young pupil shouted racist abuse to another child?

WOULD I KNOW WHAT TO DO IF … ?

A fight broke out in the school canteen?

A student blew cigarette smoke into my face when I told them to stub it out?

I overheard two students planning to bunk off the next lesson?

I was supervising a group alone and an angry student chased another out of the room shouting 'I'm gonna kill you, you b - - - - - d'?

A student made homophobic remarks to a fellow classmate?

■ OHT 7.3: DEVELOPING POSITIVE LANGUAGE SKILLS

This section reinforces the importance of using positive language skills to:

- model respect
- convey an expectation of compliance
- reduce confrontational dialogue
- convey empathy
- teach appropriate behaviour.

OHT 7.3 provides a list of language tools for positive behaviour management. These can be discussed as a group. Facilitator notes are provided below.

COMMUNICATE HIGH EXPECTATIONS IN TERMS OF COMPLIANCE

A simple but extremely effective use of language when giving pupils an instruction is to use 'thank you' rather than 'please'.

For example, instead of saying 'Can you two stop talking please!' try using 'I need you both to stop talking now, thank you'. The use of 'thank you' conveys the message that you expect the pupils to comply with your instruction. You are thanking them in advance, whereas the reliance on 'please' can be interpreted as a form of pleading or sarcasm, depending on the way it is said.

KEEP THE FOCUS ON APPROPRIATE BEHAVIOUR

Help pupils to be clear about what it is we require of them. School or classroom rules are usually written in a positive fashion (we will be kind to others) but this is not always transferred to our verbal communication. By focusing on what we don't want the pupils to do, we may be reinforcing the behaviour and encouraging others to join in. Instructions like 'Stop chatting' and 'Don't run just to get there first', will be less effective than, 'You need to listen now thank you' and 'Walk to the door in a mature and sensible way'.

ACKNOWLEDGE THE PUPIL'S FEELINGS

Always remember that challenging behaviour is a form of communication. By acting-out, the pupil may be communicating the fact that he/she doesn't understand the work, is tired, bored, feels threatened, is worried or upset, feels shown up or hard done by, etc. A quiet word of acknowledgement can sometimes be helpful, but avoid saying 'I know how you feel'. Instead, say something like:

- 'Maybe you do think this is boring but we still need to get it finished this lesson'
- 'I can see that David has upset you. Would you like to talk to someone about it?'
- 'It looks as though you could do with some help to get started?'

COACH AND ENCOURAGE

It is unrealistic to expect all pupils to be able to just adopt and exhibit appropriate behaviour in school without some help. Just as some pupils have difficulty in their learning and require structured help and support, the same is true of behaviour.

POSITIVE LANGUAGE SKILLS

- **Communicate high expectations in terms of compliance**

  Use 'thank you' rather than 'please'.

- **Keep the focus on appropriate behaviour**

  Say what it is you want rather than don't want.

- **Acknowledge the pupil's feelings**

  Remember that behaviour is a form of communication.

- **Coach and encourage**

  Recap, clarify objectives, model and demonstrate, offer positive feedback and critically review.

Effective support is about being proactive rather than just reactive (OHT 7.4). The following structure can be helpful:

- *Recap* – 'OK, before we go in, let's just remind ourselves of the rules we have in history lessons/assembly.'

- *Clarify objectives* – 'What I need you to do is face the front and listen to Mr Harris without calling out.'

- *Model and demonstrate* – courtesy, good manners and consideration. Also, give encouragement by saying things like: 'Remember how pleased we were with you last time? You managed it then so I know you can do it again.'

- *Offer positive feedback* – immediate non-verbal signals such as nod, frown, smile. Verbal reminders such as: 'What should you be doing?' or 'Well done for remembering!'

- *Review* – find something positive to say: 'I noticed you put your hand up twice in that lesson, well done.' Always focus on the target behaviour that you set out to coach: 'Did you manage to face the front and listen without calling out? What was the hardest thing to manage? How can we improve that?'

◼ HANDLING ARGUMENTS

During our daily interactions with pupils, it is not uncommon for some pupils to verbally challenge, answer back or try to manoeuvre staff into defending their instructions or requests. It is very easy to get drawn into arguments with pupils in this way. Ask team members to share some of their experiences, from home or school. There are a number of strategies that can be used to minimize the chances of getting drawn into arguments with pupils. These are illustrated on OHT 7.5 and can be used as a basis for discussion. Role-play exercises can be a very effective way to rehearse these skills and some teams will feel comfortable enough to have a go at Activity 7.3. No public performance is required! It just provides an opportunity to rehearse some techniques. Alternatively, encourage the team to try them out at home!

▶ ACTIVITY 7.3: ROLE PLAY EXERCISE – HANDLING ARGUMENTS

Photocopy scenarios 1–4

Ask colleagues to work with a partner that they feel comfortable with and give a complete set to each pair. The cards should then be divided up between them so that each partner has two adult cards and two pupil cards. Make sure that no one has the same scenario number on more than one card.

Each pair decides which scenario to start with and partners then spend a few minutes reading the card without discussion or showing one another the content of their card.

When both partners feel ready, the person with the adult card initiates the role-play interaction. Emphasize that it is OK to start again if things don't go according to plan. That's the beauty of role play!

All pairs can work at the same time, in different parts of the room, to avoid audience effect.

COACHING APPROPRIATE BEHAVIOUR

First, point out what it is they are doing:

'Daniel, you are out of your seat'

(as opposed to 'What do you think you are playing at?')

Then ask these kinds of questions:

What have you been asked to do?

What's our rule about that?

How do you think that makes………..feel?

What will happen if you don't………..?

How will you feel if that happens?

What do you need to do instead?

What do you think is the sensible choice?

TECHNIQUES FOR AVOIDING ARGUMENTS

- Stay calm!

- Be aware of body language

- Lower your voice and keep tone respectful

- Be clear and concise

- Refer to the behaviour not the pupil

- Remind pupil he/she has a choice

- Put the positive choice first

- Allow time for the pupil to comply

SCENARIO 1

ADULT

You hear a 'snap' and when you turn round you see a broken ruler on the pupil's table. The pupil is looking guilty.

SCENARIO 1

PUPIL

You have been playing about with your ruler and bending it. Suddenly it snaps in half. The teaching assistant comes over but didn't see it break as their back was to you at the time. You are going to deny everything and blame someone else.

SCENARIO 2

ADULT

The pupils are doing an end-of-term assessment test. You are supervising a group in the library and you notice the pupil looking across at someone else's paper. They have all been told that they must not look at anyone else's work.

SCENARIO 2

PUPIL

You are doing an end-of-term test in the library with the teaching assistant supervising your group.

You have just finished the last question and you lean over to see whether your friend has finished as well.

SCENARIO 3

ADULT

You are working with a small group in the learning support room. There has been some light-hearted banter between a couple of boys but then one of them makes a pen mark on the pupil's (your role-play partner's) sleeve. They respond angrily, shouting 'Oi ! You f...ing idiot!'

SCENARIO 3

PUPIL

You are in the learning support room working with a group and the teaching assistant. You have been having a bit of a laugh but then one of the boys goes too far and makes a biro mark on the sleeve of your new shirt. You are devastated and call him a 'f...ing idiot'.

The teaching assistant goes for you instead of him!

SCENARIO 4

ADULT

You arrive back from swimming with the class later than usual because the bus was delayed. The pupil walks past you in the cloakroom and goes into class with their coat on. The rule is that all coats are removed and hung up in the cloakroom.

SCENARIO 4

PUPIL

You arrive back at school after swimming. The bus was 20 minutes late picking you all up and it is now 3 p.m. School ends at 3.20 p.m. It is not worth taking your coat off so it makes sense to keep it on.

TEAM POST-SESSION PLAN

UNIT 7: DEVELOPING STRATEGIES FOR EFFECTIVE BEHAVIOUR MANAGEMENT

What aspects of positive behaviour management do we need to work on as a whole team?

1.

2.

3.

Actions to be taken:

INDIVIDUAL POST-SESSION PLAN

UNIT 7: DEVELOPING STRATEGIES FOR EFFECTIVE BEHAVIOUR MANAGEMENT

Task for the next session

REFLECTIVE LOG

UNIT 7: DEVELOPING STRATEGIES FOR EFFECTIVE BEHAVIOUR MANAGEMENT

What have you learned about your own style of behaviour management?

What strategies for positive behaviour management will you try to incorporate into your practice?

Setting Targets for Success

UNIT OBJECTIVES

This unit focuses on the process for setting positive and achievable targets for pupils, based upon objective and specific language and accurate assessment and recording. It emphasizes the importance of establishing small steps for learning and involving the pupil in the management of their own behaviour.

The objectives of the unit are:

- to enhance skills in analysing behaviour
- to promote a consistency of approach in describing, assessing and recording behaviour
- to set out a structured process for devising and monitoring individual behaviour support plans.

The session activities are designed to support the teaching assistant to:

- develop skills in using objective and specific language to describe behaviour
- develop skills in identifying, observing and recording behaviour
- understand the process of target-setting using SMART targets
- develop skills in supporting and monitoring individual behaviour plans.

PRIOR TO THE SESSION

Ask team members to complete the pre-session task sheet. They should think of one particular pupil who displays challenging or difficult behaviour. On the task sheet under column A, they should list the problem behaviours the pupil exhibits in school and under column B describe the appropriate behaviour they would like to see these replaced with. Team members should use objective and specific language to describe the behaviours.

UNIT 8 RESOURCES

Pre-session task: Identifying behaviour
OHT 8.1: The five key elements of target-setting
OHT 8.2: Observing and recording behaviour
OHT 8.3: The ways in which teaching assistants can involve pupils in target-setting
Activity 8.1: Describing behaviour
Activity 8.2: Using objective and specific language
Activity 8.3: Setting targets
Post-session activity: ABC analysis
Post-session activity: Frequency analysis
Team post-session plan
Individual post-session plan
Reflective log

SESSION MATERIALS AND AUDIO/VISUAL AIDS

- Overhead projector.
- Flip-chart sheets and pens.

NOTES FOR SENCO/TRAINER: SETTING TARGETS FOR SUCCESS

A child may display a range of complex and challenging behaviours and consequently evoke feelings of confusion in those working with them in deciding just which interventions would positively move the child forward. There may be many associated factors in the child's life that impact on the way they behave. They may be repeating patterns of behaviour that they have found rewards them with attention, however negative. They may be unaware of the consequences of their actions or yet to learn the skills to manage classroom norms. They may be fearful of experiencing repeated failure in their learning and so develop blocking strategies to protect their self-esteem.

Targets can help break down complex behaviours into manageable components that can be addressed in small learning steps. The most effective targets focus on achievable changes in behaviour that can readily be identified and made as concrete as possible to the pupil. Similarly, if the target is relatively short term, the pupil can identify the success being made and hence be motivated to move on to the next step in their learning.

THE LANGUAGE WE USE TO DESCRIBE BEHAVIOUR

If we set out targets to support pupils to modify their behaviour and learn new ways of behaving, then the *language we use* to describe the problems they present is crucially important. The problem behaviour of children is often described using adjectives or adverbs (e.g. uncooperative, aggressive, lacking concentration). These words can mean different things to different people, since they are associated with a wide range of behaviours. Similarly, vague, subjective or imprecise descriptions or statements (e.g. 'John is not motivated to learn in school', 'John is very moody' or 'John does not know how to be sensible') tell us very little about the context of the problem behaviour. In

PRE-SESSION TASK
IDENTIFYING BEHAVIOUR

Think of one particular pupil who displays challenging or difficult behaviour. Under column A, list the problem behaviours the pupil exhibits in school and under column B, describe the appropriate behaviour you would like to see these replaced with. Use objective and specific language to describe the behaviours.

A	B

order to identify specific behaviours that can be worked on with the pupil we need to reduce or eliminate perceptions, attitudes and judgements which go beyond what can be observed in the 'here and now'.

Describing behaviour as *objectively* as possible is necessary to formulate the targets to be achieved and makes the measurement of progress easier by clarifying changes that have been met.

Consider these for descriptions and statements about behaviour:

1. 'John is a spiteful little boy.'
2. 'John hurts children around him in an underhand way.'
3. 'John pinches children who sit near him.'
4. 'John pinched Abdul four times during the English lesson.'

In statement (1) we have a judgement made about John that is all-consuming and subjective; it is an unhelpful value judgement on who John is as a person and gives us no information about the problem behaviour to be addressed.

In statement (2) we have more information about what John does (he hurts children), but the qualifying phrase 'in an underhand way' is again subjective and open to interpretation, and does not give us any information about the context of the behaviour.

In statement (3) we know more about the kind of hurting John does (he pinches) and the target of his aggression (children who sit near him). What we still do not know is the *frequency* of the behaviour or the *context* in which the behaviour occurs.

In statement (4) we are given more specific information about John's behaviour – the frequency of it and the context the behaviour occurred. This is a more helpful statement that gives us a starting point to understand more about the behaviour.

If we use clear, descriptive performance language, we are in a better position to reach agreement on what the problems are and what changes are needed. We can also begin to measure behaviour – in terms of intensity, frequency and duration – and set targets for alternative or more positive behaviours for the pupil to work towards.

■ REVIEWING CLASSROOM MANAGEMENT

Prior to drawing up a specific behaviour plan for a pupil it is worthwhile to check whether more general classroom interventions can be taken to remedy the problem. Off-target behaviours of most children can be addressed within the framework of everyday classroom management.

Review the situation by asking yourself:

- Is the pupil being given work of an appropriate level?
- Has the problem behaviour been discussed with the child?
- Is the behaviour always corrected in front of others rather than in private with the pupil concerned?
- Will changing seating arrangements or other aspects of the classroom environment bring about changes in behaviour?

- Is the pupil being praised and 'caught being good'?
- Is the pupil receiving the appropriate attention and response within the class?
- Does the pupil need reminding of the class rules?
- Has advice been sought from colleagues and parents?

Having reviewed the pupil's responses to these general interventions, the next step is to define what the behaviour looks like, how often and under what circumstances it occurs, how long it lasts and who it affects. This can be achieved through observation and assessment.

OBSERVING AND ASSESSING BEHAVIOUR

Observation and assessment of pupil behaviour can provide us with a range of data that can be used to plan individual support and to set targets. The information gathered can be used to:

- identify and prioritize particular aspects of behaviour
- identify positive aspects of behaviour
- identify patterns of problem behaviour
- avoid the use of labelling and judgemental or stereotypical views
- help pupils to be more aware of their own behaviour
- enable effective target-setting
- reflect on what happens before and after the behaviour
- examine the impact of the behavior.

One model of analysing behaviour that has proved useful in school is the *ABC* format (sometimes called functional analysis) that has its roots in Learning Theory. The underlying principle of Learning Theory is that behaviour is learnt and can be changed. This behaviourist perspective maintains that people learn to behave in particular ways because those behaviours have been 'rewarded' in some way in the past.

ABC stands for Antecedents Behaviour Consequences.

Antecedents – observable environmental factors or events that precede the pupil behaviour. The probability of a behaviour occurring, is influenced by its antecedents. When considering what led up to the behaviour occurring, it can be helpful to think of this in terms of background factors as well as the immediate or proximal events that prompt the behaviour. We can think of this in terms of:

- stimulus – the immediate precursor or trigger. Are there specific triggers that can be observed prior to the behaviour occurring? Some common triggers include not getting attention, difficulty with task, task not challenging enough, spending too long on the same activity, changes in routine, unstructured time and off-target behaviour of other pupils.
- settings – this might include aspects of the physical environment or the home environment. It may be related to longer-term physiological factors such as health or emotional state. Some settings are easy to

change; others are beyond our control. Sometimes we fail to take account of the settings because we are so used to them that we take them for granted (e.g. curriculum or organizational factors).

When looking at antecedents it is important to consider whether problem behaviour occurs at certain times of the day or in particular locations. Look for patterns. Do problems arise in playtime but not at lunchtime? With Mr X but not with Mrs Y?

Behaviour – observable and identifiable behaviour.

Consequences – observable events that follow on from the observed behaviour. When we talk about consequences, in ABC analysis, we are not just referring here to sanctions or punishments such as time-out or detention. The consequences can be anything that shapes or influences the behaviour. They can be events that are rewarding or punishing (positive or negative reinforcers). Some consequences may reward pupils inappropriately. For example:

A – the teacher asks for silence.

B – Sophie coughs very loudly.

C – the rest of the class laugh.

Although the teacher gives Sophie a disapproving look and shakes her head, Sophie repeats the behaviour the next time the teacher asks for silence. By laughing at Sophie's behaviour, the rest of the class provided what is known as the 'payoff' and, in this example, the pay-off outweighed the teacher's disapproval.

Although ABC analysis can be undertaken in an informal observation through everyday classroom interactions, its potential to provide relevant data is greater if specific time is allocated. In this way the person doing the observation can give full focus to what is happening in the classroom, to the pupil's responses and to the impact the behaviour has on the pupil and others.

An ABC analysis log is included in the post-session activity.

A *frequency analysis* can be undertaken to observe the frequency of on-target and off-target behaviour over a given period (e.g. 30 minutes of a lesson). The observer notes the frequency of the pupil's behaviour on a regular basis, every five minutes for example, and records what the pupil is doing. In this way, the regularity and pattern of the behaviour can be observed and an intervention planned that responds to the frequency of the behaviour. A frequency analysis log is included in the post-session activity.

◼ SETTING TARGETS

The data collated from the observations can then be analysed and used as a basis for setting targets. Again, the language used in setting out the targets is an important factor for its success. If targets are phrased positively (i.e. in terms of what we want the pupil to achieve) the pupil is more likely to recognize its attainment as a personal achievement. This can be done by writing the targets as 'Paul will … ' rather than 'Paul will not … '.

As we have discussed earlier, there may be many problem behaviours that require support, however, it is not possible to tackle all of the behaviours at the one time. Deciding which behaviours to prioritize, or to initially target, will depend on a number of factors:

- The priority behaviour, although very worrying, may be an infrequent occurrence.
- The pupil will need to experience achieving success with other targets in order to build up confidence to attempt a more direct behavioural target.
- The pupil's developmental level – the pupil may need to develop more skills in specific areas before directly tackling the major difficulties.
- You may not yet feel confident in tackling particular areas of behaviour management.
- The antecedents are already known and pertain to issues being addressed in other contexts (e.g. child protection, family breakdown, etc.).

It is advisable to set the pupil no more than two or three targets at any one time. The pupil can easily become overwhelmed if there are too many targets set and, consequently, lose interest or be unable to distinguish the priorities. The targets should be monitored and reviewed at regular intervals.

Targets should be SMART:

Specific – describes, using objective language, what the pupil will be able to do.

Measurable – the expectations are quantified and the success criteria is outlined.

Attainable – the targets are broken down into small steps that do not overwhelm the pupil.

Realistic – the targets are based on accurate observation and assessment and relate directly to the pupil's level of development and skills; targets are realistically resourced and supported.

Time-limited – the pupil can achieve the target in the time frame given and experience success.

Monitoring of the targets should be undertaken on a regular basis; for some pupils this may be on a lesson by lesson basis and for others on a daily or weekly basis. A specific named person should take responsibility for monitoring the targets, issue any rewards or stickers for achieving set targets and keep a record of progress. Self-monitoring sheets and booklets can motivate pupils to keep on track and then collated in their record of achievement file to show evidence of progress.

INVOLVING PUPILS IN TARGET-SETTING

Pupils are more likely to achieve targets for their behaviour if they are fully involved in the target-setting process itself. Involving pupils in writing and reviewing targets is an essential part of supporting them to take responsibility and ownership of their behaviour and to develop the skills of self-reflection. Pupil involvement can take many forms – taking part in formal review meetings, informal individual discussions and in circle time activities. The ultimate objective of a behaviour plan is to enable self-control to take over from teacher or external control.

STRUCTURE OF THE SESSION

A suggested structure is as follows.

Notes for OHT 8.1

THE FIVE KEY ELEMENTS OF
TARGET-SETTING
Explain the five key elements and
highlight specific areas that teaching
assistants are presently involved.
Give examples of existing good
practice.

THE FIVE KEY ELEMENTS OF TARGET-SETTING

1. Identifies and prioritizes specific behaviours through observation and assessment

2. Identifies appropriate interventions, resources for support and time allocation

3. Focuses on what the pupil can achieve taking small steps

4. Can be quantifiable and measurable

5. Involves the pupil in taking responsibility for their own behaviour

▶ ACTIVITY 8.1: DESCRIBING BEHAVIOUR

Hand out Activity 8.1 sheets and go through the first statement as an example with the whole team. In small groups or pairs ask the team to consider the rest of the statements on the sheet and rate them in terms of objectivity/subjectivity and specificity/generality. Discuss responses.

DESCRIBING BEHAVIOUR

Ask the team to consider the following statements and then rate them in terms of **objectivity/subjectivity** (column 1) and **specificity/generality** (column 2).

	Obj 5 4 3 2 1 Subj	Spec 5 4 3 2 1 Gen
1. Alvin can't be bothered to learn.		
2. James interrupted the teacher five times in ten minutes.		
3. Georgia finds it difficult to follow a complex set of instructions.		
4. David can be quite violent in the playground.		
5. Paulo tends to disturb the other pupils in his group.		
6. Vicky cries for ten minutes every morning when she first arrives at school.		
7. Meera likes to be the centre of attention.		
8. Lena is sensible and mature.		
9. Hal kicked Thomas twice at lunchtime and then spat on his plate.		
10. Tom calls out the answers instead of putting his hand up.		

▶ ACTIVITY 8.2: USING OBJECTIVE AND SPECIFIC LANGUAGE

In pairs ask the team to (a) choose two of the most subjective descriptions from Activity 8.1 and rewrite them to make them more objective, and (b) choose two of the most general descriptions and rewrite them to make them more specific. Collate responses and write up on flip chart. Discuss changes. Do the statements identify more clearly the behaviour to be targeted?

USING OBJECTIVE AND SPECIFIC LANGUAGE

Choose two of the most subjective descriptions from Activity 8.1 sheet and rewrite them to make them more objective

1.

2.

Choose two of the most general descriptions from Activity 8.1 sheet and rewrite them to make them more specific

1.

2.

Notes for OHT 8.2

OBSERVING AND
RECORDING BEHAVIOUR

Discuss with the team the different elements
involved in observing and recording behaviour.
Give out copies of the ABC analysis and frequency analysis sheets (post-session activity)
and discuss. Emphasize how the more objective and specific the behaviour is described, the
easier the target can be identified and written.

OBSERVING AND RECORDING BEHAVIOUR

Use objective and specific language to describe the behaviour

Consider the antecedents and consequences of the behaviour

Observe and record the behaviour using ABC analysis and frequency analysis

Set SMART
<u>S</u>pecific
<u>M</u>easurable
<u>A</u>ttainable
<u>R</u>ealistic
<u>T</u>ime-limited targets

Monitor progress on a regular basis and involve the pupil

▶ ACTIVITY 8.3: SETTING TARGETS

Ask the team to choose two of the behaviours they identified on the pre-session activity sheet and write a SMART target for each one. When completed, ask team members to share with a partner. Write up the targets on the flip chart and discuss as a team.

SETTING TARGETS

Choose two of the problem behaviours you have identified in the pre-session task and write a SMART target for each one.

Use objective and specific language.

Phrase the target in a positive way, e.g. PAUL WILL………………..

Problem behaviour	Target

Notes for OHT 8.3

WAYS IN WHICH TEACHING ASSISTANTS
CAN INVOLVE PUPILS IN
TARGET-SETTING

Discuss the approaches suggested on the OHT
with the whole team. Can the team add other
approaches they have used? Which are the
areas for development?

WAYS IN WHICH TEACHING ASSISTANTS CAN INVOLVE PUPILS IN TARGET-SETTING

- One-to-one discussion

- Circle time activities

- Self-monitoring sheets and booklets

- Review meetings

- Joint meetings with parent and pupil

- Assemblies and tutorial time

> ▶ POST-SESSION ACTIVITY
>
> Plan a timetable for all members of the team to observe and record a pupil's behaviour using the ABC analysis log and/or the frequency log.

ABC ANALYSIS

ANTECEDENTS	BEHAVIOUR	CONSEQUENCES

FREQUENCY ANALYSIS

FREQUENCY (minutes)	BEHAVIOUR
5	
10	
15	
20	
25	
30	
NOTES	

TEAM POST-SESSION PLAN

UNIT 8: SETTING TARGETS FOR SUCCESS

What aspects of the observation, recording and target-setting process do we need to work on as a team?

1.

2.

3.

Actions to be taken:

INDIVIDUAL POST-SESSION PLAN

UNIT 8: SETTING TARGETS FOR SUCCESS

Task for the next session

REFLECTIVE LOG

UNIT 8: SETTING TARGETS FOR SUCCESS

How does your knowledge and understanding of the observation, recording and target-setting process help you in your Teaching Assistant role?

What implications might it have for future practice?

ADDITIONAL RESOURCES

Further useful information may be obtained from the following web sites and journals. (It should be noted that the views and recommendations contained in these resources are not necessarily endorsed by the authors)

Websites

Additional Needs Net
http://www.additionalneeds.net

ADDNet
http://btinternet.com/~black.ice/addnet

Anti-Bullying Network
http://www.antibullying.net

Antidote – Campaign for Emotional Literacy
http://www.antidote.org.uk/

Association of Workers for Children with Emotional and Behavioural Difficulties
http://www.awcebd.co.uk/

Becta Ebd Forum
http://www.search.ngfl.gov.uk/ebd-forum/

Behaviour Change Consultancy – UK
http://www.behaviourchange.com

Citizenship Foundation
http://www.citfou.org.uk

Database of initiatives for working with EBD children in the mainstream classroom
http://www.users.globalnet.co.uk/~ebdstudy/choose.htm

Department for Education and Skills
http://www.dfes.gov.uk/sen/

Framework for Intervention (Birmingham City Council)
http://www.f4i.org

Inclusion – catalogue of resources
http://www.inclusion.ngfl.gov.uk/

Jenny Mosley's Quality Circle Time
http://www.circle-time.co.uk

Kidscape
http://www.kidscape.org.uk/

Kids Online
http://www.kids-online.org.uk/

The Mental Health Foundation
http://www.mentalhealth.org.uk/

The National Association for Special Educational Needs
http://www.nasen.org.uk

National Children's Bureau
http://www.ncb.org.uk

National Emotional Literacy Interest Group
http://www.nelig.com/

National Society for the Prevention of Cruelty to Children
http://www.nspcc.org.uk/

The Nurture Group Network
http://www.nurturegroups.org

Self Esteem Advisory Service
http://www.selfesteemadvisoryservice.com

School of Emotional Literacy
http://www.schoolofemotional-literacy.com

Talking Teaching – best practice forum
http://www.talkingteaching.co.uk/

TeacherNet (DfES)
http://www.teachernet.gov.uk/professionaldevelopment/opportunities/nqt/
behaviourmanagement/classroombehaviour/

Team-Teach – training provider
http://www.team-teach.co.uk

Journals

Behavioural Disorders
Beyond Behaviour
British Journal of Educational Psychology
British Journal of Special Education
Child and Adolescent Mental Health
Educational Psychology Review
Emotional and Behavioural Difficulties
European Journal of Special Educational Needs
Exceptional Children
Focus on Exceptional Children
International Journal of Inclusive Education
Journal of Behavioural Education
Journal of Educational Psychology
Journal of Emotional and Behavioural Disorders
Journal of Positive Behaviour Interventions
Special Children
Support for Learning

Index

Special Needs and Early Years

A Practitioner's Guide

Kate Wall *Canterbury Christ Church University College*

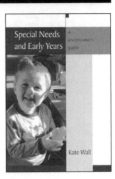

'This well crafted "practitioners guide" thoughtfully addresses the many issues that practitioners race when they consider their involvement in early education in the context of work with special educational needs. Those who read this book will find that they know a little more about these important issues and may find themselves challenged to reflect on their personal attitudes towards inclusive education: ideally becoming better providers for children with learning difficulties'-
Cathy Nutbrown, Journal of Early Childhood Research

'This is an exemplary introductory textbook for students, and a veritable mine of information. Undoubtedly, this is an early years/special needs book that many readers can and will relate to' - *Sheila Wolfendale, European Journal of Special Needs Education*

'This is Kate Wall's first book and, in my view an excellent one. Anchored within the framework of inclusion, it provides a clear focus on under-fives with special educational needs. The author's concentration on pre-school children reflects her opinion that there already exists a plethora of information about children who have attained statutory school age.

Above all, **Special Needs and the Early Years** is a true practitioner's guide. Kate Wall draws on her extensive experience and proven skills, supplementing them with personal observation. She combines these skillfully with current theory and thoughtful reflection to produce an impressive and coherent work, one that I thoroughly recommend' -
British Journal of Special Education

Research in early years and special needs shows the need for early and appropriate intervention. But not all early years practitioners have the expertise, knowledge and skills to ensure these expectations are transformed into high-quality special needs provision.

Kate Wall believes that all children should be entitled to achieve their full potential, and that all practitioners should have the necessary skills to support children and their families. Her extensive work as a teacher in mainstream and special early years settings, combined with her current senior lecturing experience, has helped her to identify the key issues for practitioners and parents including: working with families; partnerships with parents; observation and assessment; programmes of intervention; and responding to the affective needs of children.

Having spent many years supporting families of children with special needs she now shares her expertise in an accessible book based on her own research and practice. The book offers practical suggestions for working practice and in-service training.

This book is essential reading for early years practitioners, professionals dealing with special needs children and their families, and students in the early years and special needs fields.

March 2003 • 198 pages
Cloth (0-7619-4075-8)
Paper (0-7619-4076-6)

Autism and Early Years Practice

A Guide for Early Years Professionals, Teachers and Parents

Kate Wall *Canterbury Christ Church University College*

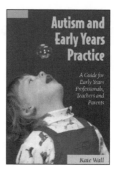

With every early years setting now expected to be more inclusive, early years professionals are increasingly working with children who have autism or who appear on the autistic spectrum.

This book is written with the needs of the practitioner firmly in mind. It offers advice based on the author's own experience as a practitioner and provides the reader with sound knowledge of the area which will support and inform practice. Useful, practical, realistic and constructive suggestions will be made by exploring research and current examples of good practice; these will be supported by individual case studies as exemplars. Each chapter will highlight key issues, offer suggestions for discussion and direct the reader to key texts for further reading.

Subjects covered include:

· definitions of autism

· the demands of relevant legislation

· considering the needs of the family

· issues of diagnosis and assessment

· understanding the world of the child with autism

· programmes of intervention

· including young children with autism

· working effectively within a multi-disciplinary system

· current issues and suggestions for the future

All early years students and professionals working with children in a variety of early years settings will find this book helpful and closely matched to their needs.

Kate Wall is Early Childhood Studies Programme Director at Canterbury Christ Church University College. She has worked extensively as a practitioner in early years mainstream and special needs settings.

April 2004 • 168 pages
Cloth (1-4129-0127-8)
Paper (1-4129-0128-6)

Encouraging Positive Behaviour in the Early Years

A Practical Guide

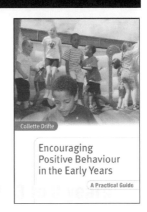

Collette Drifte

By offering clear guidance and plenty of suggested strategies, **Encouraging Positive Behaviour in the Early Years** provides the reader with a framework for encouraging positive behaviour from all young children.

Sections include:

· the revised SEN Code of Practice 2001 and the Disability Discrimination Act 2002 and their implications for practitioners

· strategies for encouraging positive behaviour and reducing inappropriate behaviour

· planning, writing and reviewing Individual Education Plans (IEPs)

· working with colleagues to write and implement a positive behaviour policy.

There is a range of photocopiable material provided, as well as some practical activities that would be useful when delivering INSET in any early years setting. Suggestions for further reading are made and a glossary of terms is included.

Nursery teachers, nursery nurses, all those early years professionals working in the private sector, teaching assistants, students working towards NVQs, tutors of early years courses, childminders and playgroup workers will find this book highly readable and suited to their needs.

April 2004 • 144 pages
Cloth (1-4129-0135-9)
Paper (1-4129-0136-7)